GERONIMO
and
The End of The Apache Wars

Geronimo at Fort Sill, 1898. The painting is by E. A. Burbank (courtesy, Arizona Historical Society).

Geronimo

and The End of The Apache Wars

Edited by C. L. Sonnichsen

University of Nebraska Press
Lincoln and London

First Bison Book printing: 1990
Most recent printing indicated by the first digit below:
10   9   8   7   6   5   4   3   2   1

Library of Congress Cataloging-in-Publication Data
Geronimo and the end of the Apache wars / edited by C. L. Sonnichsen.
p.   cm.
Published also as v. 27, no. 1 of Journal of American history.
This Bison book edition omits "Eve Ball, in memoriam" by Lynda Sanchez.
ISBN 0-8032-9198-1
1. Geronimo, Apache Chief, 1829–1909. 2. Apache Indians—Wars, 1883–
1886. 3. Apache Indians—Biography. 4. Indians of North America—Southwest, New—Biography. I. Sonnichsen, C. L. (Charles Leland), 1901–
E99.A6G3243   1990
979′.004972—dc20
[B]
89-24966 CIP

Reprinted by arrangement with the Arizona Historical Society

Originally published as a bound, limited edition of the Spring 1986 issue of
the *Journal of American History*, Volume 27, Number 1. This Bison Book edition
omits "Eve Ball: In Memoriam" by Lynda Sanchez.

∞

CONTENTS

Naiches + Geronimo.

FOREWORD

This book commemorates one of the most significant events in the history of the Southwest—the surrender of Naiche, the hereditary Chirichahua chief, and Geronimo, the Apache shaman and war leader, to General Nelson A. Miles at Skeleton Canyon on the Mexican border on September 4, 1886. It was the end of an era—the beginning of a new day for the white man and of bitter exile for the Indians. The documents and articles which follow are intended to throw light on the personalities and events which changed the course of history in the Territory of Arizona a century ago.

GERONIMO
and
The End of The Apache Wars

FROM SAVAGE TO SAINT
A New Image for Geronimo

by

C. L. Sonnichsen

LIFE IS ALMOST OVER FOR CHOKOLE, an Apache woman warrior. She has been defeated and captured in a battle with Mexican soldiers high in the Sierra Madre in northern Mexico. Badly wounded, she has been staked out on an anthill while unconscious and left to die slowly and horribly. Her body is suppurating. Ants are working on her decaying tissues and on her eyes. Four buzzards are hopping closer.

Chokole was about to close her eyes when a swift shadow shot over the ledge. The shadow alarmed the buzzards. They stumbled away, jumping and hopping, flapping into the air. Chokole looked up from the shadow. It was a great eagle. He was tilting, turning against the wind and coming back. This time, he stretched taloned feet and braked against the air, landing close to Chokole. She saw him turn his head, looking at her. He kicked at the sand on the ledge. Chokole blinked her eyes. It was Geronimo.[1]

This is the Geronimo we all know, the once-notorious Apache, transformed and transfigured by the imagination of novelist Forrest Carter. He has become, for Carter, an Indian George Washington who battles the United States Army to a standstill with a handful of warriors; an Apache Moses who, under instructions from Jesus Christ to Chokole just before the eagle arrives, leads the remnants of his band to a Promised Land—a hidden valley in the mountains of Mexico. His people

Formerly Chief of Publications of the Arizona Historical Society and Senior Editor since 1977, C. L. Sonnichsen came to Arizona after retiring as professor and dean at The University of Texas at El Paso. His specialty is western fiction, which he treats as social history.

[5]

suspect that he is "a Shaman of War returned from the past"[2] and credit him with the ability to predict future events and to know about other happenings going on far away.[3]

Carter goes even farther. When Mexican troops surround the band, hiding in a thicket, and light a circle of fires, Geronimo summons a whirlwind to put the fires out so the Indians can escape.[4] His extraordinary powers come into play on one of his flights from the reservation. Wanting to know if he is being pursued, he sits down under a bush and watches the plants around him.

> Softly Geronimo chanted. Not words, but tones that matched the rhythm of their harmony. The tones were soothing and beautiful, rising and falling without break or abruptness. The rhythm became stronger, a haunting odor came to his nostrils from the leaves of the creosote bushes. The burro bushes moved their branches in unison to the chant. Slowly Geronimo felt the rhythm tightening. Were the danger moving from them, the rhythm would have lengthened, growing more languid. Now, faintly, breaks of excitement came, staccato; and he knew the soldiers had not stopped. They were coming.[5]

To Forrest Carter, Geronimo is an Indian Messiah. The Apache wars are a "heroic struggle" by "a small group of people resisting the attempts of two powerful governments to enslave and exterminate them," and Geronimo is a great leader "fighting for his people's right to live free."[6] The white men are the villains, their cause is "thievery, plain and simple."[7]

Carter's novel is the culmination of a process which has been going on for a full century—a process in which Geronimo has undergone a desert change and become a symbol of heroic resistance. In the 1880s he was a symbol of just the opposite, of murderous bloodlust and ruthless cruelty. Strangely enough, the two Geronimos have existed side by side almost from the beginning, and they still so exist, but Geronimo the Wicked is barely alive in the second half of the twentieth century, and Geronimo the Good is having things pretty much his own way. How could such a reversal have taken place? This is how it happened.

In the 1880s, when Geronimo and his braves were terrorizing southern Arizona and northern Mexico, the man was evil

[6]

Geronimo smiling—a rare occurrence. San Antonio, 1886.

personified. General Nelson A. Miles, who eventually accepted his surrender, ranked him chief among the "worst, wildest and strongest" of the Indians.[8] General George Crook, a friend of the Apaches, branded him as a "human tiger."[9] John P. Clum, Indian agent at San Carlos and the only man who ever "captured" Geronimo, thought the country would be better off if Geronimo were hanged.[10] In Oklahoma a generation or two later, according to a pioneer's granddaughter, "When my mother was growing up, people said to their children, 'If you don't behave, Geronimo will get you.' "[11]

Although he never led more than a handful of effective fighting men, he was credited with wholesale slaughter. In 1900, fifteen years after his last break-out in 1885, *Outing* magazine still believed the worst:

> Seventy-six white men, women and children were killed by Geronimo in his last raid. It is said that in the years 1869 and 1870 one hundred and seventy-six persons were murdered by his band of Apaches, and according to a record kept by Herman Ehrenberger [Ehrenberg], a civil and mining engineer, four hundred and twenty-five persons, at that time one half the American population of Arizona, fell victim to the scalping knives of Geronimo's braves between 1856 and 1862.[12]

This was giving the devil a good deal more than his due, since Geronimo was only a minor figure until the eighties, overshadowed by Victorio, Mangus Colorado, and Cochise.

The Apache menace, however, was very real to the settlers. Historians now discount the outrage of the pioneers and the hysterics of the newspapers, attributing ulterior motives to the merchants and editors as they demanded more soldiers to chase Indians and bring more business to Arizona and New Mexico. To the white people involved, this would have been utter nonsense, convinced as they were that the lives of every man, woman, and child in the territories were in deadly peril.

They made this clear when on April 30, 1871, William S. Oury and Juan N. Elías of Tucson led 148 Mexicans, Papagoes, and Anglos in perpetrating the notorious Camp Grant Massacre. Over 100 Apaches, mostly women and children, were surprised

[8]

at daybreak and slaughtered. The rest of the country was appalled and demanded that the slayers be punished, but an Arizona jury refused to convict them.[13] Oury, first president of the Arizona Pioneers Historical Society, defended his actions before a large and appreciative assembly of members and guests on April 6, 1885. The Apaches, he said, "had held a carnival of murder and plunder in all our settlements." Then came that "glorious and memorable morning," and when every adult Indian had been done to death, the men ate breakfast "in the full satisfaction of a work well done."[14]

To men and women who accepted the Camp Grant Massacre as an act of self preservation, it was impossible to regard Geronimo with anything but hatred and loathing. When he left the San Carlos Reservation in 1882 and again in 1885, something like mass hysteria gripped the citizens of Arizona and New Mexico, and the whole country watched with horror and incredulity as the Apache raiders looted, murdered, and burned on their way to hideouts in the Mexican mountains while soldiers, scouts, and civilians pursued them in vain. Editors screamed for aid from Heaven and Washington.[15] Newspapers and magazines in California and the East picked up the chant. The temper of the times was demonstrated when in 1885 General George Crook seemed to be succeeding in his efforts to bring Geronimo out of Mexico and confine him again on the desolate San Carlos Reservation. A mass meeting in Tombstone declared: "If Crook brings these murderous scoundrels back to the reservation and turns them over to the civil authorities again . . . it would be a heroic act for the people of Arizona to massacre every one of them."[16]

Outsiders reinforced the prevailing opinion. Charles Fletcher Lummis came to Fort Bowie in 1886 to report on the final throes of the Apache campaigns and described the Apache as a "born butcher." "From time untold he has been a pirate by profession, a robber to whom blood was sweeter than booty — and both as dear as life." Of Geronimo Lummis was inclined to be scornful, describing him as "a talker from jawville," though not "the biggest fighter, the biggest schemer nor the bloodiest raider in the outfit at any time till now . . . . The only claim Geronimo has to his unearned pre-eminence of newspaper notoriety is that he is one of the originators of the outbreak." Still, Geronimo was an Apache, "whetted down to a ferocity of edge unattainable by" other Indians.[17]

Geronimo, then, was no freedom fighter in Arizona in 1886, and his people were seldom thought of as human beings. They were unclean savages, crafty, cruel, elusive and embarrassingly efficient as warriors but incapable of any refinement of thought or conduct. The Mexicans called themselves *gente de razón*—people of reason—in contrast with the *bárbaros*. Every bad trait that the white people recognized in themselves, they automatically pinned on the Apache. He smelled bad, had no manners, enjoyed watching human and animal suffering, and the truth was not in him.[18]

The image of the Apache as a perfidious, ruthless, bloodthirsty savage endured, though eventually with diminishing emphasis, until the third quarter of our century. In the early years books written by Army personnel and by their wives and daughters kept the negative image of the Apache alive. All the important people involved in the pursuit and surrender of Geronimo left their memoirs—Crook, Miles, Britton Davis, John G. Bourke, and even Anton Mazzanovich, an enlisted man with a long memory. To all of them the Apaches were "the hostiles," and Geronimo was the great enemy, though they respected him as a resourceful field commander, a "wily savage" who kept several thousand troops, several hundred Indian scouts, and numerous civilians busy and frustrated until relentless pursuit wore him out.

The historians went along. Paul I. Wellman in 1935 described him as "cunning, bloodthirsty, and his cruelty was a bottomless pit."[19] In 1938 Frank C. Lockwood, professor and scholar, called him "a man of immense courage, energy and effrontery...a cruel, perfidious rascal, hated and distrusted by Apaches and white men alike."[20] Dan Thrapp in *The Conquest of Apacheria* (1967) wrote with considerable objectivity, but he was not about to make a hero of Geronimo, referring to him in passing as one of several "doughty recalcitrants" and commenting on his "baleful influence."[21]

It was for the novelists, however, that Geronimo provided a marvelous opportunity. He and his people made wonderful vil-

Before crossing the border Geronimo (beside horse) poses with his band.

lains. Edward S. Ellis wrote several cheap novels about the Apache campaigns, including a crude paperback, published in 1901, called *On the Trail of Geronimo,* in which a young officer, just out of West Point, fights the "dusky fiends" of the Southwest, led by Geronimo himself.[22] In the same year Gwendolyn Overton, daughter and wife of Army officers, published *The Heritage of Unrest,* a significant novel about a half-Apache girl brought back to Arizona from schooling in the East, white in her upbringing but unable to throw off the "taint" of her Apache blood. She has no feelings of compassion, likes to watch wild creatures fight, and wields a deadly knife when a white man attacks her. She gives her life for her husband, however, and Mrs. Overton can't resist approving of her as the story develops.[23]

Captain, later General, Charles King, an Army novelist with fifty-nine titles to his credit, knew the Apaches at firsthand. A West Pointer, he was ordered to Arizona in 1870 and was severely wounded in a fight with the Tontos in 1874. Using his Army experiences as raw material, he became a popular

[11]

storyteller, setting a dozen novels and short stories in Arizona.[24] His main interest is in garrison life and in the romantic entanglements of his young lieutenants, but the Apaches are never far away and eventually must be dealt with in the field. In *An Apache Princess* (1903) a chief's daughter falls in love with the handsome lieutenant and pursues him with savage persistence until he introduces her to his white sweetheart. Then, "with the spring of a tigress she bounded away."[25] Like Felipa in *A Heritage of Unrest*, she is handy with a knife. King doesn't really know much about Apaches, except that they can be dangerous and that "they truckle to no man."[26]

King was a sentimentalist, but he served up some Apache atrocities. In *Sunset Pass* (New York: Lovell, 1890) the Tontos toss a captive into a wagon and burn them up together. Mrs. Overton and her successor Forrestine Cooper Hooker (*When Geronimo Rode*, 1924) were gentle and refined ladies, however, and did not dwell on such horrors. The novelists who followed them had no such scruples. In the 1950s James Warner Bellah, a retired Colonel with an Eastern background, gave the Apaches credit for every kind of wickedness. His warriors are animals, "blood-drunk and beast-hot. Reeking to defile. Hair-tearing hands, grease slick. Fetid-breathed and shrieking with foul obscenities."[27] There is no hope for a white woman who falls into their hands. "You have to see it to believe what they do to white women. There is a ferocity in it that beggars rationalization... the Indian in his free-running state is only a step up from the beast. He is lecherous and without honor or mercy, filthy in his ideas and speech and inconceivably dirty in his person and manners. They had caught Detweiler's wife and grown daughter in their beds. Their faces were beaten blue, their flank flesh was clawed to ribbons. Their gibbering must finally have gotten them killed."[28]

Summing it all up, Bellah writes:

It can be a phase of the moon that maddens Apaches, or a word from the memory of a medicine chief, or a strange flower by the trailside, or an omen of blood in a stone; because the Apaches hate life and they are the enemies of all mankind.[29]

[12]

It would be interesting to observe the outcome if Bellah had ever decided to pay his respects to Geronimo. But he never did. The old warrior crops up from time to time, however, in other "westerns." In the 1970s he was still needed to head the "renegades" so there could be a chase and a buildup of suspense. The "wily old butcher" appears in Lewis B. Patten's *The Hands of Geronimo* (1971) as he leaves the reservation and heads for Mexico in 1885. He waylays a stage carrying Elizabeth Romero, her son Jimmy, and her baby.

Before it got to Globe the Apaches attacked it. . . . They killed the driver and the guard. They killed all the passengers and thought they had killed Elizabeth. They crushed the baby's head by dashing it on one of the wheels. And, maybe on a whim, they took Jimmy along with them.[30]

Jonas Railey, a cowboy who loves Elizabeth, joins Lieutenant Britton Davis's cavalry troop in pursuit and eventually gets Jimmy back.

Somewhere between 150 and 200 paperback westerns have dealt with the Apache wars, and Geronimo is a character in many of them, often under his own name but more often under another, and the names are suggestive: Tucsos, Chingo, Natano, Soldado, The Butcher, Diablo, Diablito, Satanio. The chief is always a mighty and mysterious leader who outthinks and outmaneuvers his white adversaries, able in subtle ways to influence their minds and, in modern idiom, to "psych them out." His face is the face of Geronimo as captured by a photographer at San Carlos in 1884. "The face was one that might look from a smoky window of hell, a beaked nose, a thin slit of lipless mouth."[31]

Natano neither glanced at him nor spoke nor changed his expression. . . . Behind the small, crafty eyes in a square, flat face were plans and schemes and dreams. By the wrinkles which seamed his skin like etchings on leather, one recognized age, wisdom, and experience; in the unyielding, slitted mouth one saw determination. In the eyes and mouth and bone of this face was ruthlessness, a cruelty ages old.[32]

[13]

*The earliest known photo of Geronimo, taken by photographer
A. Frank Randall at San Carlos reservation in 1884. This is the face
that launched a hundred articles, stories, and novels.*

[14]

In the fourth quarter of our century, Geronimo the Menace appeared only infrequently in paperback novels, but his legend lingered on. Responding to the increasing appetite for gore and violence, popular fiction writers made capital of the qualities attributed to him in earlier times and even found new ways to induce suffering and death. A good example would be the Cuchillo Oro series by William James (a pen name for Englishman Terry Harknett), featuring a huge, formidable, and ruthless Apache with a golden-hilted knife—a *cuchillo de oro*. His wife and child have been murdered by white soldiers, and he seeks and finds revenge. In *Sonora Slaughter* (number 6 in the series), he flips out the eyes of a bounty hunter with his knife, then castrates the man in order to impress a Mexican bandit who has him covered, and finally rapes a captive woman in the presence of the gang as a clinching bid for survival and acceptance.[33] The publisher announces on the cover of the books that the Apache Series is "inspired by such notorious Indian warriors as Cochise and Geronimo."

Thus Geronimo the Wicked has survived until our time.[34] But the other Geronimo, Geronimo the Hero, has more than kept up with him. The first signs of change came when he was in full career. The entering wedge was the consciousness that the Indian, including the Apache, had been abused and betrayed by the white man. Humanitarian spokesmen after the Civil War transferred their efforts from the black man to the red man. Wendell Phillips and William Lloyd Garrison led the van, attacking the Army for slaughtering Indians. "I only know the names of three savages upon the Plains—Colonel Baker, General Custer, and at the head of all, General Sherman." These were the sentiments of Wendell Phillips in 1870.[35]

People in the East, particularly people who had never been West or seen an Indian, were convinced that sweet reasonableness would bring the Indian troubles to an end. Westerners, of course, were nauseated by such silly simplicity, but the beginnings of our national guilt complex over our treatment of the First Americans was sometimes visible, even in the West. One can see it starting in 1901 in *Heritage of Unrest*. Mrs. Overton comments on Apache-White relationships:

He was a simple, sullen Apache, and his untutored mind could only grasp effects. Causes were beyond it....He knew that the stores which should have gone to him were loaded upon wagon trains and hurried off the reservation in the dead of night; but he did not know why the Apache who was sent to humbly ask the agent about it was put in the guard house for six months without trial. He knew that his corn patches were trampled down, but not that it was to force him to purchase supplies from the agent or his friends, or else get out. He has not yet learned to take kindly to financial dishonesty. Does he owe you two bits, he will travel two hundred miles to pay it. He still has much to absorb concerning civilization.[36]

Geronimo could never be a hero to Mrs. Overton, and his people would never be more than "simple, sullen savages." The first real effort in fiction to make a human being out of an Apache came with Harold Bell Wright's *The Mine with the Iron Door,* a romance set in the Santa Catalina Mountains near Tucson. In the second rank of characters is an educated Apache named Natachee, a solitary outcast. His education unfits him for tribal life, and his Indian blood excludes him from any close connection with the whites. The degradation of his people by the predatory newcomers grieves him, and he sees the hopelessness of the Apaches' situation:

"You tell me that I should teach my people how to live? By that you mean that I should teach them the ways of the white people? Is it the duty of one who has been robbed of all that was his to accept the thief as his schoolmaster and spiritual guide? . . . Could you expect one who has been humiliated and shamed and broken to set up the author of his degradation as his ideal and pattern? . . . For gold your people destroy the forests — tear down the mountains — dry up or poison the streams — lay waste the grass lands and bring death to all life. For gold they would rob, degrade, enslave and kill every race that is not of white blood. . . . By this same gold for which the Indian peoples have been destroyed shall the Indians be revenged; for by this gold shall the destroyers themselves, in their turn, be destroyed.

"There is nothing left for the Indian but to die. I, Natachee, have spoken."[37]

Four years later, in 1927, it was Geronimo's turn. Edgar Rice (Tarzan) Burroughs published the first of his two novels

[16]

with Geronimo as an important character. The focus is on Shoz-di-ji-ji, Black Bear, a white boy who has won great distinction as a warrior, believing himself to be a full-blooded Apache. His hatred for the White Eyes knows no bounds, and he has fought them close and hard. Geronimo—gentle, old, and wise—still hopes for peace and wants Shoz to stay away from the white man and his property. Shoz is indignant.

"The Black Bear makes his camp where he will, hunts where he will."

"Those are the big words of a young man, my son," said Geronimo. "It is fine to make big talk, but when we would do these things the soldiers come and kill us; every white-eyed man who meets our hunters upon the trails shoots at them. To them we are as coyotes. Not content with stealing the land that Usen gave to our forefathers, not content with slaughtering the game that Usen put here to feed us, they lie to us, they cheat us, they hunt us down like wild beasts.... Go-yat-thlay is not afraid to die; but he does not like to see the warriors and women and children slain needlessly, and so he waits and hopes—hopes that the Pindah-lickoyee will some day keep the words of the treaties they have made with the Shis-Inday—the treaties they have always been the first to break.[38]

In Burroughs's book we see the Apache for the first time as a freedom fighter, a peace-loving, home-loving, independent desert dweller, violent only in defense of his life and land. The whites are the villains, greedy and perfidious. Already Geronimo is becoming a symbol of resistance to arrogant and overwhelming might.

It is worth noting that the acid test for the Friends of the Apache is intermarriage. The basic question is, "Would you want your daughter to marry one?" The taboo is a mighty one, and the most humanitarian of the revisionists has trouble getting around it. To Charles King the love of his Indian "princess" for the white officer is almost ridiculous. Felipa's first marriage to a white man in *The Heritage of Unrest* is without love, and both her marriages are terminated by the death of the man. Even when a mixed marriage is allowed, it cannot be permanent. Approved Indian-white intermarriage was many years away in 1933, when Burroughs published

[17]

Apache Devil, his second Black Bear novel. Unfortunately for his peace of mind, Shoz falls in love with a white girl and makes no progress.

"If Shoz-di-ji-ji was a white-eyed man, you would listen," he said.
"Oh God, I don't know," she cried.
"Shoz-di-ji-ji knows. . . ." He wheeled his pony and rode away.[39]

Not until Geronimo reveals his white parentage does poor Shoz make headway with Wichita Billings.

Other Apaches replaced Geronimo in the spotlight as the thirties and forties rolled by. Will Levington Comfort's *Apache* (1931) made an admirable and impressive human being out of Mangus Colorado. Edwin Corle tried to understand a less admirable but no less embattled Apache in *Figtree John* (1934), and Paul I. Wellman in *Broncho Apache* (1936) pays tribute to Massai, who escaped from a train bearing him to prison camp and returned to the old wild life in Arizona. Other Indians from other tribes were getting similar favorable treatment. Meanwhile the Roosevelt administration, with John Collier as Commissioner, was giving the Indian back his land, upgrading his lifestyle, and restoring his vanishing culture. Now that the Apache was no longer a threat, crowds of investigators, amateur and professional, descended upon him, notebooks in hand, and the great revolution in attitudes was under way. Like buckets in a well, the white man went down as the Indian went up. By 1965, when Thomas Berger published *Little Big Man,* "brutish soldiers rampage about the West gleefully slaughtering peaceable Indians and taking special delight in shooting down helpless women and children."[40]

It was the same in Geronimo's Arizona, and 1947 was a climactic year in bringing the new picture into focus. In that year Elliot Arnold published his best-selling novel *Blood Brother,* a great success in the United States and England—a success which continued with its transformation into the motion picture *Broken Arrow.* It is the story of Tom Jeffords, a mail contractor and Army scout who was a close friend of Cochise. At Cochise's insistence he served as Agent for the newly created Chiricahua

[18]

Geronimo (left) and Naiche as cowboys on the reservation at Fort Sill. Geronimo autographed this photo.

Reservation when the tribesmen agreed to stop raiding and settle down. In Arnold's novel the whites are far inferior to the Apaches. Jeffords, speaking for Arnold, says:

"There is no private hoarding, no cheating. Whatever they have is divided equally.... There's no caste system, and no aristocrats and no commoners.... How did people in one part of the world just naturally develop the king idea and the people of another just never did? ... We talk about Indian princesses. There never was an Indian princess.... Despite our boasts we just cannot conceive of any people being inherently democratic.
"I wonder by what standards we have arrogated to ourselves the right to call Indians savages.... Who are we to come along and try to make them over our way?"[41]

If the Apache has attained this elevated status in the eyes of his white brothers, what about the taboo against interracial marriage? Even for novelist Arnold, it still holds. Jeffords marries Son-see-ahray, a ward and relative of Cochise, and enjoys an idyllic honeymoon with her, but their happiness is short lived. She is shot in the back by rascally white men and dies with her unborn child.

The taboo still operates in Jane Barry's *A Time in the Sun* (1962). Anna is on her way to marry her soldier fiancé in Arizona when she is captured by Apaches. Their lifestyle pleases her, and she falls in love with half-Mexican Joaquín. They discuss Indian "atrocities."

"They burned a man. Burned him."
He said, "Have you ever seen Apache scalps on Mexican and American saddles? Have you seen them geld and flay our wounded? Or what they do to our dead if we don't recover them?"[42]

Anna and Joaquín marry, but their happiness must be cut short. This time it is the man who has to go. Joaquín dies at the hands of skulking whites.

A number of hard-cover novels in the seventies are sympathetic to the Apaches and their cause, usually conceding that a minority of restless and vindictive Apache malcontents caused all the trouble.[43] Two recent novels and one nonfiction account focus on the Camp Grant Massacre, not one of them defending the attackers.[44] Even the later paperback novels show signs of generosity toward the Apaches. Al Sieber, Crook's chief of scouts and a man with no delusions about the situation, is sometimes the spokesman. In Lewis B. Patten's *The Hands of Geronimo* he comments:

"All in all, I'd say it was a goddam stinkin' mess that nobody can do much about. The easiest way out seems to have escaped everybody."
"What's that?" I asked.
"Treat 'em right. See that they got food and clothes enough to keep 'em warm. Let 'em live in the mountains around Fort Apache where they've always lived. Stop pushin' 'em around."[45]

Hunter Ingram in *Fort Apache* (1975) takes the campaign a few steps farther.

Tydings stared straight ahead. "This may shock you, Owen, but... what we're doing to the Apaches is as cold-bloodedly brutal as anything the Apaches can think of.... Have you ever stopped to realize that the Caucasian race is the scourge of the earth? The Apache kills on an individual basis. The white race kills on a mass basis.... They plan to wipe out whole cultures at once."[46]

Since these ideas and attitudes have become standard, the most notorious of the Indian leaders could hardly escape being upgraded. He appears in the novel before Lieutenant Owen Parnell with other unhappy Apaches who are planing to leave the reservation. They are resentful because they have been forbidden to make and drink *tiswin* and to discipline their wives. "But that isn't what is really troubling you," says the lieutenant.

The blaze in Geronimo's eyes rekindled with a new fury. "I am weary of being cheated, of being treated like a dog. All the promises given to me have turned out to be lies. I am weary of seeing my people hungry and sick."[47]

According to the novelist, Geronimo is fully justified. Captain Emmett Crawford explains to Owen that the Indian agents and the Tucson Ring of crooked merchants, working together, are robbing the Indians blind and starving them to death.

"I've seen some bad Indian agents, but Tiffany is a new low. My God, it makes you want to puke.... Go into any nearby town and you can find Apache supplies being sold openly.... Hell, yes, the Ring wants another Apache outbreak. Then they can scream to Washington for more protection. That would mean more fat contracts.... This is the damndest nest of vipers I ever stepped in."

"Why shouldn't Geronimo be discontented?" Crawford asks. "He can do better off the Reservation."[48]

The existence of a Tucson Ring has never been proved, and there is evidence that it was never a reality,[49] and it seems, furthermore, that poor, fat, slow-witted Agent John C. Tiffany has been wrongly crucified,[50] but fiction writers need villains, and the Ring and the Agents have replaced the Apaches as the people to hate. Motion pictures reinforced the point for non-readers in such films as *Broken Arrow* (1950) and *Battle at Apache Pass* (1952), in both of which Geronimo appeared.[51]

With the dawn of the 1980s Geronimo seems to have lost all his ferocity and become something like a middle-class American business executive. An example is James A. Bryan's *Savages* (1983). Ryan Flynn, prospecting in the Superstition Mountains, is robbed and left for dead by a white rascal posing as a preacher. He is rescued and nursed back to health by a lovely Apache girl, a sister of Geronimo, who takes him home and marries him. Flynn defends the Apaches against the white crooks who are stealing from them and becomes a close friend of Geronimo, who speaks good English and behaves like an outgoing, generous Christian gentleman until white men take his land and murder his relatives. Then he goes on the warpath.[52]

Factual writers in the 1960s and 1970s marched side by side with the novelists, giving a receptive public the noble savage, the abused aborigine, the sadistic soldier, the venal bureaucrat, the misguided missionary, the soulless civilian, riveting the shackles of what Robert Utley calls "the white man's guilt over his historic treatment of the Indian."[53] At the same time the

Geronimo as farmer—in his watermelon field at Fort Sill.

western tribes, encouraged and represented by white lawyers, anthropologists, and Indianists, petitioned the government for millions of dollars to compensate them for lost lands and won their cases, while commentators of all complexions were giving the Indian his due and considerably more. Sentimentalists like T. C. McLuhan (*Touch the Earth*, 1976) glowed over the Indian's kinship to his environment. Serious historians like Virgil Vogel (*This Country Was Ours*, 1972) and Wilbur Jacobs (*Dispossessing the American Indian*, 1972) show how the Indian has been victimized. Popular historians like Dee Brown (*Bury My Heart at Wounded Knee*, 1971) and Stan Steiner (*The Vanishing White Man*, 1976) convinced many thousands of readers that the cause of the Indians was just and the record of the white conquerors was shameful and criminal. It became almost an article of faith that we stole the country from the red men, who were wild and free with an admirable lifestyle and a noble pantheistic religion; that we caged them, starved them, lied to them, took their country away from them, and tried to exterminate them in the name of progress. There was, of course, plenty of evidence to support this view and prepare the way for Vine Deloria, an educated Indian who declared in ringing tones that the white man had exploited the country almost out of existence and would have to return to the Indian way if he hoped to survive. "Within the traditions, beliefs, and customs of the American Indian people," he said, "are the guidelines for mankind's future."[54] John Upton Terrell gave the coup de grace to the ignoble white man in 1972:

> Through the years ... superior American military power gradually drove the Apache closer to the end of their tether, but it never succeeded in completely defeating them. That was accomplished by the perfidy, the treachery, the inhumanity of bestial white civilians both in Washington and the Southwest, forces which created in them a hopelessness they were unable to combat.

. . . .

It should be understood that almost every Spanish and Mexican *colono* and ordinary American who sought his or her fortune in the Apache country stood low on the social scale, a great many of them the dregs of their respective societies. There were among them very

[24]

few persons of education, and an even smaller number with any type of professional training, and not very many possessed social amenities acceptable any place that ranked above a bawdy-house waiting room. The vast majority . . . were uncouth, ignorant, bigoted and looking for something for nothing.[55]

Only a few historians like Robert M. Utley (*Frontier Regulars: The U. S. Army and the Indians 1866-1890*, 1973), Robert W. Mardock (*Reformers and the American Indian*, 1971), and Francis Paul Prucha (*American Indian Policy in Crisis*, 1976) had anything good to say about white people dealing with Indians on the frontier. To most sensible, truth-seeking citizens in our country in the second half of our century it seems that the pro-Indian, anti-white stance "is the only view that is historically defensible."[56]

The transformation of Geronimo and his Apaches into something rich and strange was aided and furthered by Geronimo himself, though he had no such outcome in mind, through the publication of his autobiography in 1906.[57] S. M. Barrett, a superintendent of schools in a town near Fort Sill, where the Apaches had found a home, decided that he had a priceless opportunity to record Geronimo's recollections before the old man passed on. After a good deal of negotiation with the government (Geronimo was still technically a prisoner of war), Barrett won approval and began seeing Geronimo regularly, with Asa Daklugie (a cousin) acting as interpreter. The interviewer was not allowed to ask questions. "Write down what I tell you," Geronimo said. The book could have been much better, but it turned out to be in some ways a very important volume, "the first account of the Apache wars from the inside looking out,"[58] and it was enormously useful to writers who came along in the decades that followed. Geronimo gave an account of his childhood, his growing up and training as a warrior, and the terrible events in his young manhood (the murder of his young wife and children) which made him bitter and vindictive. His reminiscences became the basis for a number of books for young people, holding young Geronimo up as a role model for white American boys. In them he appeared as a sort of All American Boy while he was in training, and then as

[25]

a resourceful leader in his early manhood. At least seven of these books were published in the United States and England.[59]

Another ingredient in the mixture which produced Geronimo the Good and Great was introduced by anthropologists and students of Indian culture. They learned that Geronimo was not a hereditary chief, but was a powerful shaman who could do things that no ordinary Apache could do. This did not mean that he as a medicine man ministered to the needs of his fellow tribesmen as a white doctor ministers to his patients or a white preacher ministers to the needs of his congregation. There was power in nature, and any man could command some of it. The power was individualized, and a man's Power would give him a ceremony which he could use for the benefit of others with specific needs. If something went wrong for an Apache, he would enlist the services of a man or woman with an appropriate ceremony.[60]

Geronimo's Power was particularly strong and helpful, and his fellow tribesmen gave him credit for extraordinary abilities. Some of them were able to give examples. Jason Betzinez, for example, tells about something that happened in Mexico:

> We were sitting there eating. Geronimo was sitting next to me with a knife in one hand and a chunk of beef which I had cooked for him in the other. All at once he dropped the knife saying, "Men, our people whom we left at our base camp are in the hands of United States troops. What shall we do?"[61]

It turned out that Geronimo was right. At other times he predicted future events correctly,[62] and on one occasion he delayed the sunrise when his people were crossing open ground at night. "So he sang, and the night remained for two or three hours longer. I saw this myself."[63]

Put all these elements together and you have something almost irresistible to non-Indians under peril or stress. In Paris Geronimo's people and example appealed so successfully to the French underworld that a collection of shady or semi-shady characters called themselves *Les Apaches,* and people came from far and near, even from America, to view them in their native haunts. During World War II paratroopers hurled themselves into space shouting, "GERONIMO," as Texans used to

[26]

Geronimo selling bows and arrows. St. Louis World's Fair, 1904.

cry, "Remember the Alamo."[64] The name was a sort of incantation, embodying such slogans as "All or Nothing," "Shoot the works," or "Do you sons of bitches want to live forever?"

Geronimo cropped up again in California when the street people of Berkeley took over a vacant lot belonging to the University of California and called it the Power to the People Park. They were unwelcome to the university administrators and were asked to leave. They refused and passed out a leaflet bearing a photograph of Geronimo and the words, "Your land title is covered with blood. Your people ripped off the land from the Indians. If you want it back now, you will have to fight for it."[65] There were no Indians among them, but by this time Geronimo was not a man but a symbol which belonged to everybody.

We have even come to the place where we can contemplate adopting Geronimo as an example of the American spirit. "The spirit of the Apaches," says one of Geronimo's biographers, "lives wherever men and women are struggling against overwhelming odds for freedom and justice. We, as Americans, should be proud that the Apaches' story is part of our country's heritage."[66]

With this background Geronimo-as-Prophet in Forrest Carter's *Watch for Me on the Mountain* can be better understood. It is still astonishing that this transformation has taken place, but it is not without precedent. Pancho Villa comes to mind as another Great Rogue who became a Great Hero, and Wyatt Earp, a rather pathetic saloon-and-gambling-hall figure whom Stuart Lake made over into a plains-and-desert Galahad, is another. But Geronimo's transformation goes beyond the others. Carter uses every device to make him credible and sympathetic. First he gives him an extraordinary grievance. Geronimo himself tells about the murder of his family by Mexican troops, but Carter brings the scene before his reader's eyes:

Goklayeh first saw his mother, broken, old eyes glazed at the sky. Near her, the bloody round flesh ball that was his baby. His eyes followed the dark trail of Leta over the rocks where she reached to touch the foot of her mother, Alope; by her side the headless body of

[28]

Tala curled, seeking and finding the mother comfort. One hand of Alope's was outstretched, reaching for the baby. She was gone. Alope was gone. They were all gone.[67]

Next Carter makes him a victim. He is being brought to San Carlos in chains by John Clum:

He was filthy. Excrement had caked and dried on his pants. Naiche knew he had been in the hole. His hands were bound with chains, and the soldiers led him by a rope looped around his neck.

They passed close to the bush and Naiche stood stoically, not looking at the soldiers, only at the man. Bushy hair fell down about the prisoner's bowed head, but as he passed, he turned his face slightly. His eyes fastened full on Naiche's. The eyes gave no evidence of his humbled condition; they flashed black and fanatical. He said nothing. He was Geronimo.[68]

Naturally Geronimo rebels against this sort of treatment, but he is more than a righteous rebel. He is a philosopher who has a deep spiritual understanding of the whole situation. Carter does not allow Geronimo to explain the Indian religion, but Tom Horn does so to General Crook.

"Well, the 'Pache believes if you keep the high laws, then you strengthen your spirit body. Each time you git on the wheel . . . that is, git born again into a material body on earth, you exercise these high laws against the *low* laws that the material world goes by. Now, as you strengthen your spirit body, then each time you die—or pass from this material world—your spirit body is stronger . . . if you done it right . . . kept the faith and all . . . and you move to higher and higher plateaus. The highest plateau, naturally, is the one where you're so strong, you don't have to come back.[69]

When Geronimo asks for his sister Ishton's life, his Power reminds him of his religion:

"You chose to come back to the earth world and place your spirit body in conflict with the forces of the lower planes. You chose, Geronimo, to strengthen your spirit body. You may keep the faith with your spirit or you may weaken and surrender your soul to the lower planes. You

Geronimo enters the machine age. Time: June, 1905. Place: the Miller Brothers' Ranch, Indian Territory. Occasion: convention of the National Editorial Association. The car: a 1904 Locomobile.

may have the child to comfort you at the time your earth body is old. You may have Ishton for a short time with Juh. Ask nothing more. Only you may kill your spirit body." Geronimo answered, "I will ask nothing more."[70]

So this is what we have done with Geronimo. We have adopted him and transformed him, made him an invincible leader with supernatural powers, made him a priest and a prophet of his people, deeply spiritual and in touch with the Great Mystery, a symbol of our most heroic and unselfish impulses, an epitome of humanity at its best.

Here was a subject for poetry, and a poet appeared. Charles Fletcher Lummis, correspondent for the *Los Angeles Times* in 1886, a man with very little respect for the Apaches, responded emotionally to Geronimo in 1928 in *A Bronco Pegasus*:

> A prophet of his people, he,
> no war Chief but their Priest,

From Savage to Saint

And strong he made his Medicine
  and deep his mark he creased—
The most consummate Warrior
  since warfare first began,
The deadliest Fighting Handful
  in the Calendar of Man.[71]

In 1972 the tune and the words were different, and the jukebox gave the theme a different rhythm and resonance, but the idea was the same:

They put Geronimo in a jail down south,
  Where he couldn't look a gift horse in the mouth,
Sergeant, Sergeant, don't you feel
  There's something wrong with your automobile?

Now Jesus tells us, I believe it's true,
  The Red Man is in the sunset too.
Ripped off his land and we won't give it back.
  Send Geronimo a Cadillac.
  Oh boys take me back.
  I want to ride in Geronimo's Cadillac.[72]

Unfortunately Geronimo lived too long. He should have perished in Mexico, fighting valiantly beside his men. Since we have been at such pains to make a superman out of him, it is disturbing to learn that he spent his last years raising watermelons and vegetables at Fort Sill, Oklahoma; that he became a public spectacle at fairs and conventions, selling his signature for twenty-five cents, or a dollar if he could get it; that he sold his shirt buttons to the people who flocked to see him and carried a supply with him to sew on between stops; that he died of pneumonia brought on by lying out all night following a big drunk.[73] It would have been easier to make a Samson or a Siegfried out of him if he had moved out on the Circle of Life before he surrendered to General Miles.

[31]

NOTES

[1] Forrest Carter, *Watch for Me on the Mountain* (New York: Delacorte, 1978), p. 264. Carter, author of *The Vengeance Trail of Josey Wales,* claimed to be half Cherokee and described his imagined youth in *The Education of Little Tree* (1976). Lawrence Clayton, his only biographer to date, believes that his Indian identity was "a fictional device" (L. C. to C. L. S., April 23, 1984).

[2] Carter, *Watch for Me,* p. 83.

[3] Jason Betzinez, *I fought with Geronimo,* ed. W. S. Nye (Harrisburg, Pa.: Stackpole, 1959), pp. 90, 113.

[4] Carter, *Watch for Me,* p. 178.

[5] *Ibid.,* p. 63.

[6] *Ibid.,* pp. 199, 244.

[7] *Ibid.,* p. 53.

[8] General Nelson A. Miles, *Personal Recollections and Observations* (Chicago: The Werner Company, 1897), p. 445.

[9] General George Crook, "The Apache Problem," typescript, Gatewood Collection, Arizona Historical Society, Tucson, Box 2, Folder 5.

[10] Woodworth Clum, *Apache Agent: the Story of John P. Clum* (Lincoln: University of Nebraska Press, 1978, first published, 1936), p. 228.

[11] Carolyn Row Barber to C. L. S., May 31, 1985.

[12] "Outdoor Men and Women," *Outing* (January, 1900), p. 480.

[13] Don Schellie, *Vast Domain of Blood* (Los Angeles: Westernlore, 1968), tells the story with some objectivity. Elliot Arnold in *The Camp Grant Massacre* (New York: Simon & Schuster, 1976), takes the side of the Indians. Only Constance Wynn Altshuler in *Chains of Command* (Tucson: Arizona Historical Society, 1981), pp. 194-195, takes seriously the pioneers' contention that the Apache men were raiding.

[14] Arizona Pioneers Historical Society, Minutes, April 6, 1885.

[15] John A. Turcheneske, "The Arizona Press and Geronimo's Surrender," *Journal of Arizona History,* vol. 14 (Summer, 1973), pp. 133-148.

[16] *Tucson Daily Citizen,* June 6, 1885.

[17] Charles Fletcher Lummis, *Dateline Fort Bowie,* ed. Dan L. Thrapp (Tucson: University of Arizona Press, 1979), pp. 48-54.

[18] See C. L. Sonnichsen, "The Ambivalent Apache," *From Hopalong to Hud* (College Station: Texas A & M University Press, 1978), pp. 64-82.

[19] Paul I. Wellman, *Death in the Desert* (New York: Macmillan, 1935), p. 233.

[20] Frank C. Lockwood, *The Apache Indians* (New York: Macmillan, 1938), p. 223.

[21] Dan L. Thrapp, *The Conquest of Apacheria* (Norman: University of Oklahoma Press, 1967), pp. 170, 217.

[22] Edward S. Ellis, *On the Trail of Geronimo* (Philadelphia: John C. Winston, 1908, first published, 1901), p. 85.

[23] Gwendolyn Overton, *The Heritage of Unrest* (New York: Macmillan, 1901), pp. 23-24, 79-84, 329.

[24] C. E. Dornbush, *Charles King: American Army Novelist* (Cornwallville, New York: Hope Farm Press, 1963), is an account of King's literary output. A full treatment of his work is Oliver Knight's *Life and Manners in the Frontier Army* (Norman: University of Oklahoma Press, 1978).

[25] Captain Charles King, *An Apache Princess* (New York: The Hobart Company, 1903), p. 324.

[26] *Ibid.,* p. 92.

[27]James Warner Bellah, *Massacre* (New York: Lion Books, 1950), p. 105.

[28]James Warner Bellah, *A Thunder of Drums* (New York: Bantam, 1961), p. 6.

[29]James Warner Bellah, *Apache* (New York: Gold Medal, 1951), p. 4.

[30]Lewis J. Patten, *The Hands of Geronimo* (New York: Ace Books, 1971), p. 6.

[31]Gordon D. Shireffs, *The Valiant Bugles* (New York: Signet, 1961), p. 8.

[32]George Garland, *Apache Warpath* (New York: Signet, 1961), p. 60.

[33]William James, *Sonora Slaughter* (New York: Pinnacle, 1976), pp. 17-19, 79-80.

[34]Sonnichsen, "Ambivalent Apache," pp. 75-80.

[35]Robert Winston Mardock, *The Reformers and the American Indian* (Columbia, Missouri: University of Missouri Press, 1971), p. 69.

[36]Overton, *Heritage of Unrest*, pp. 174-175.

[37]Harold Bell Wright, *The Mine with the Iron Door* (New York: Appleton, 1923), pp. 165-166.

[38]Edgar Rice Burroughs, *Apache Devil* (New York: Ballantine Books, 1964, first published in 1933), p. 11.

[39]*Ibid.*, p. 126.

[40]Robert M. Utley, "Good Guys and Bad: Changing Images of Soldier and Indian," *Periodical: Journal of the Council on Abandoned Military Posts*, vol. 8 (Fall, 1976), p. 30.

[41]Elliott Arnold, *Blood Brother* (New York: Duell, Sloan & Pearce, 1947), p. 429.

[42]Jane Barry, *A Time in the Sun* (Garden City: Doubleday, 1962), p. 105.

[43]Examples would include Will Henry, *Chiricahua* (1972); Gail Rogers, *Second Kiss* (1972); Reuben Bercovitch, *Odette* (1973); James R. Olson, *Ulzana* (1973); and Clay Fisher, *Black Apache* (1976).

[44]Don Schellie, *Vast Domain of Blood* (1968); Don Schellie, *Me, Cholay & Co.* (1973); Elliot Arnold, *The Camp Grant Massacre* (1976).

[45]Patten, *The Hands of Geronimo*, pp. 53-54.

[46]*Ibid.*

[47]*Ibid.*, pp. 44-45.

[48]*Ibid.*, p. 45.

[49]Floyd Fierman, "The Spectacular Zeckendorfs," *Journal of Arizona History*, vol. 22 (Winter, 1981), p. 400.

[50]John Bret Harte, "The Strange Case of John C. Tiffany," *Journal of Arizona History*, vol. 16 (Winter, 1975), pp. 383-404.

[51]Jon Tuska, "The Post War Indian," in *The Filming of the West* (London: Robert Hale, 1978), pp. 533-538, discusses the changing role of the Indian in moving pictures.

[52]Robert Vaughn, *Savages* (New York: Dell, 1983).

[53]R. M. Utley, "Good Guys and Bad," p. 30.

[54]Vine Deloria, Jr., *God Is Red* (New York: Delta Books, 1973), p. 300.

[55]John Upton Terrell, *Apache Chronicle* (New York: World, 1972), pp. xi-xii.

[56]Gregory McNamee, review of Evan S. Connell's *Son of the Morning Star*, in *Tucson Weekly*, April 3-9, 1984, p. 12.

[57]S. M. Barrett, *Geronimo's Story of His Life* (New York: Duffield, 1906).

[58]Angie Debo, *Geronimo: The Man, His Time, His Place* (Norman: University of Oklahoma Press, 1976), p. 5.

[59]Therese O. Deming, *Cosel with Geronimo on his Last Raid* (Philadelphia: F. A. Davis Co., 1958); Edgar Wyatt, *Geronimo the Last Apache War Chief* (New York: Whittlesey House-McGraw-Hill, 1952); Jim Kjelgaard, *The Story of Geronimo* (New York: Grosset & Dunlap, 1958); Ralph Moody, *Geronimo: Wolf of the Warpath* (New York: Random,

1958); Geoffrey Bond, *Geronimo Rides Out* (London: Arco Publications, 1962); Matthew D. Grant, *Geronimo: Apache Warrior* (Mankato, Minn.: Creative Education, Distributed by Children's Press, 1974); Ronald Syme, *Geronimo the Fighting Apache* (New York: Morrow, 1975).

[60]Morris E. Opler, *An Apache Life Way* (New York: Cooper Square Publishers, 1965), pp. 200-216.

[61]Jason Betzinez, *I Fought with Geronimo*, p. 113.

[62]*Ibid.*, p. 90.

[63]Opler, *An Apache Life Way*, p. 216.

[64]How the paratroopers came to use Geronimo's name as a battle cry is yet to be explained.

[65]Stan Steiner, *The Vanishing White Man* (New York: Harper & Row, 1976), pp. 124-125.

[66]Alexander B. Adams, *Geronimo* (New York: Berkeley, 1971), p. 23.

[67]Carter, *Watch for Me*, p. 101.

[68]*Ibid.*, p. 5.

[69]*Ibid.*, p. 241.

[70]*Ibid.*, p. 134.

[71]Charles Fletcher Lummis, *A Bronco Pegasus*, p. 41.

[72]"Geronimo's Cadillac," copyright 1972 by Mystery Music, Inc., BMZ.

[73]Debo, *Geronimo*, pp. 400-405.

CREDITS—The photograph on page 7 is from the Historical Collections, Security First National Bank; on page 11 from the Gatewood Collection, Arizona Historical Society, Tucson, and on page 30 from AHS general collections; on page 14 from the National Archives and Records Service; on page 19 from the Bureau of American Ethnology Collection, Smithsonian Institution National Anthropological Archives; on page 23 from the Fort Sill Museum, Fort Sill, Oklahoma; on page 27 from the Smithsonian Institution National Anthropological Archives.

"I HAD LOST ALL"
Geronimo and the
Carrasco Massacre of 1851

by

Edwin R. Sweeney

Eearly in the morning on Wednesday, March 5, 1851, Colonel José María Carrasco, commanding Sonora's armed forces, led an army of 400 men, the majority national or volunteer troops, across the Sonoran boundary into Chihuahua. His prey: the Chiricahua Apache bands living near Janos under a peace agreement consummated on June 24, 1850. The warriors, the Sonorans believed, were responsible for recent atrocities committed in their state. Carrasco's army succeeded in surprising at least two rancherias, killing twenty-one Apaches (including Yrigollen, a principal Chiricahua chief) and capturing sixty-two. The incident created an uproar among Chihuahuan officials, who protested the Carrasco action on the ground that the Indians were residing in peace at Janos and had not raided into Sonora. The Sonoran invaders viewed all the Apaches as hostile, and consequently the innocent (and there were some) had to suffer with the guilty.

It seems likely, in spite of discrepancies in the accounts of the massacre, that Geronimo's mother, wife, and children were

Born in Boston, Edwin R. Sweeney received a degree in Accounting from the University of Massachusetts (Amherst) and is currently employed as comptroller of Silk Screen Products, Inc., at St. Louis, Missouri. He has a special interest in Arizona Apaches and is completing a book-length study of Cochise.

[35]

among the victims and that his lifelong hatred of all Mexicans was the result of this loss.

He remembered it all as an old man — the great tragedy of his early life. His band was at peace, he said, with Mexicans and with other Indians. They had camped near a village which the Apaches called Kas-ki-yeh on the banks of a little river not far from Casas Grandes in Chihuahua. The men had gone into town, leaving their families with a small guard.

Late one afternoon when returning from town we were met by a few women and children who told us that Mexican troops from some other town had attacked our camp, killed all the warriors of the guard, captured all our ponies, secured our arms, destroyed our supplies, and killed many of our women and children. Quickly we separated, concealing ourselves as best we could until nightfall, when we assembled at our appointed place of rendezvous — a thicket by the river. Silently we stole in one by one, sentinels were placed, and when all were counted, I found that my aged mother, my young wife, and my three small children were among the slain.[1]

Completely devastated, Geronimo watched the others leave for Arizona. He was as if paralyzed, "hardly knowing what I would do. I had no weapon, nor did I hardly wish to fight, neither did I contemplate recovering the bodies of my loved ones, for that was forbidden." Finally he followed the survivors, arriving at last at the old camping place in the Arizona mountains, but everything had changed for him. From that time on, whenever he thought of what he had lost, "my heart would ache for revenge upon Mexico."[2] His revenge, as history shows, was ample.

Can Geronimo's recollections be trusted? Probably only in part. He lost his family but not, it would seem, at the time and place, or under the circumstances he described when he dictated his autobiography in 1906, and in his desire to present himself as an innocent victim, he ignored the long series of raids and reprisals which preceded Carrasco's attack. It is hard to believe that he was not involved in them.

In the 1830s and 1840s the Chiricahuas[3] devastated northern Chihuahua and Sonora. Their incursions seemed to increase in severity every year after the breakdown of Mexico's presidio

Nacori Chico, Sonora, a typical isolated Mexican village, close to Apache haunts in the Sierra Madre. Photo taken about 1900.

system in the spring of 1831.[4] By the late 1840s the war parties had virtually depopulated the northern frontier of Sonora. From 1831 through May, 1848, their raids had forced the abandonment of twenty-six mines, thirty-nine haciendas, and ninety-eight ranches in the State of Sonora alone. In the District of Arizpe, the haciendas of San Bernardino, Cuquiarachi, Batepito, Pilares, Teras, San Nicolás, and Cuchuta were all deserted because of the ferocity and frequency of the raids.[5] Geronimo's statement that his people were at peace with everyone is not the whole truth.

Sonora could do little to stem the tide. Throughout the 1840s revolution and anarchy prevailed. The opposing political factions, the followers of Manuel María Gándara and of General José Urrea, fought each other instead of the Indians. The federal government in Mexico City, like the state government of Sonora, suffered from corruption, internal disputes, and incipient bankruptcy. Few troops garrisoned the north, and those soldiers who served were poorly trained, ill-equipped, and infrequently paid.

[37]

The frontier endured a further setback in mid-1849 when many able-bodied men emigrated to the California gold fields, thus depleting the state's manpower and weakening the National Guard.

In the late 1840s the Chiricahuas continued their sanguinary raids, aimed at depopulating Sonora's northern frontier. On December 23, 1847, a band of Chokonen assaulted Cuquiarachi, a small town located six miles southwest of Fronteras, killing nine men and six women, capturing six others. One month later the remaining citizens deserted Cuquiarachi for Bacoachi,[6] some thirty miles southwest of Fronteras. Two months after that Miguel Narbona led a Chiricahua war party that obliterated the town of Chinapa, killing twelve, wounding six, and capturing an astonishing forty-four. Before leaving, they burned the town.[7]

During the summer of 1848 Chiricahua war parties terrorized the people of Fronteras, who were too frightened to work their fields. As a result, the citizens and troops were starving by August and were forced to abandon their homes and move to Bacoachi.[8] One month later the military commander at Santa Cruz wrote that his troops were deserting and warned that the presidio would suffer the same fate as Fronteras if the "continuous successes of the savages are not checked."[9]

The situation could hardly have been worse for the Mexican people, and yet the Chiricahua victories in 1848 were surpassed by those of the following year. In the winter and early spring Chokonen leaders Miguel Narbona, Yrigollen, and Esquinaline joined with the omnipotent Chihenne leader Mangas Coloradas[10] and ravaged Sonora, extending their raids deeper into the interior. On January 12, 1849, they massacred a force of twenty Sonorans near Ures, the state capital.[11] Later that month Chiricahuas slaughtered thirty-five people at Cumpas and captured several citizens.[12] In that same month the inveterately hostile Miguel Narbona led 100 Chiricahuas in an attack on the mining town of Banamichi, thirty miles south of Arizpe, killed fourteen, captured twelve, and burned several haciendas.[13]

These episodes foreshadowed future events. In the spring of 1849, Chokonen and Bedonkohe war parties boldly attacked Sonora's remaining northern presidios of Santa Cruz, Bacoachi, and Bavispe, killing at least twelve people, wounding several, and capturing nine others.[14] Between April, 1849, and April, 1850, some 941 citizens from the district of Arizpe and 1216 from the district of Moctezuma emigrated to California.[15] The lure of gold influenced many of them, no doubt, but the terror of the Apaches was also a potent force.

In late 1848 Mexico took steps to restore its faltering military organization and counteract the Apache menace. In November Colonel José María Elías González, an experienced, Apache-wise campaigner, was appointed military inspector of Sonora in charge of the presidios.[16] In the same year the governor named José Ignacio Terán y Tato (another indefatigable Indian fighter) to take command of the national troops.[17] Neither man could perform miracles, and meager resources meant meager results. Nonetheless, through 1849, González and Terán y Tato channeled their energies into organizing a force to campaign in Apacheria and punish the hostiles in their rancherias.

They met with small success. They killed a few Indians, retrieved some livestock, and penetrated the Apache homeland as far as what is now southeastern Arizona. They did accomplish one thing, however: they convinced the Chiricahuas that they were no longer safe in their mountain fastnesses. This, coupled with the arrival of American troops in New Mexico, tipped the scales, and the Apaches decided to start peace talks with the Mexicans. By the early spring in 1850, the majority of the Chiricahuas had relocated in northern Mexico. The Chokonen, with the Bedonkohe under Mangas Coloradas, opened negotiations at Santa Cruz and Bacoachi, Sonora.[18] Meanwhile, the Chihenne and Nednhi bands, disturbed because nineteen of their kinsmen had recently been captured and were held in confinement at Janos,[19] talked truce at that antiquated presidio located in northwestern Chihuahua.

After a few months of negotiations the talks stalled because Sonora refused to provide the Indians with rations. Finally, after months of procrastination, state officials reluctantly acquiesced to this demand but by then the Chiricahuas' patience had waned, and they had resumed their old raiding patterns.

In Chihuahua, the Chihennes and Nednhis had few prob-

[39]

lems in reaching an agreement for an armistice at Janos. On June 24, 1850, the treaty was signed with Delgadito, Ponce, and Coleto Amarillo acting as the Apache spokesmen and leaders. Within a few weeks, the majority of the Chihenne and Nednhi bands established their rancherias within an eight-mile radius of Janos.[20] They were subsequently joined by some of the hostile Chokonen under Yrigollen. Nonetheless, the more intractable and suspicious Chokonen, Chihenne, and Bedonkone, led by Miguel Narbona and Mangas Coloradas (said to be enraged at his associates who made peace), recalling an earlier doublecross at Galeana[21] in 1846, elected to remain in the mountains in present-day southern Arizona and New Mexico.

Geronimo was almost certainly with these hostiles who continued to rob and murder in Sonora. In September, 1850, Mangas Coloradas led a large Chiricahua war party striking settlements along the Santa Cruz River.[22] Geronimo calls Mangas "our chief" at the time of the massacre. There is at least a strong possibility, Geronimo's nature being what it was, that he was with Mangas on some of these bloody raids into Sonora.

As 1850 ended, however, a year in which Apaches murdered a reported 111 Sonorans—two episodes occurred which would dramatically affect future events. The first was a peace effort by the hostiles which began in November and continued into early 1851. They wanted rations and peaceful settlement at Janos, and on several occasions Esquinaline, Teboca, and Mangas Coloradas sent emissaries to the peace commissioner, Juan José Zozaya. Each time, however, he rejected their solicitations, insisting that they first make peace with Sonora.[23]

The second event was in direct response to Governor José Aguilar's pleas for federal assistance against the Apaches. On December 21, 1850, the administration in Mexico City appointed as commanding general and inspector of the military colonies an energetic, capable, but highly controversial figure who thought himself omniscient, Colonel José María Carrasco.[24] He replaced the popular José María Elías González, who had reinvigorated and reinforced the frontier presidios and dealt as effectively as any man could with the Apaches, considering the lack of money and resources and the chaotic political situation.

[40]

Apaches in ambush for unsuspecting prospectors is the artistic subject of this card print by Buehman and Hartwell of Tucson.

Before the arrival of the new commander in Sonora, Mangas Coloradas, with some of the supposedly peaceful Apaches at Janos, organized another raid into Sonora. In early January Candelario, a son of the famous chief Juan José Compa, brought news to Janos of the campaign. Meanwhile Coleto Amarillo, leader of the peaceful Nednhis, assured Peace Commissioner Zozaya that his band would remain quiet. But other groups — Yrigollen's Chokonen and Delgadito and Ponce's Chihennes — joined Mangas. According to Sonora's official reports, two war parties, each with at least 200 warriors, raided the state. Evidently Mangas led one; Yrigollen and Posito Moraga the other.

In mid-January the raiders retired northward, driving some 1300 head of cattle and horses before them. Their route was predictable, and Captain Ignacio Pesqueira[25] gathered a force of 100 nationals from Arizpe and Bacoachi and headed for a place called Pozo Hediondo (Stinking Wells) some twenty miles east of Arizpe and a few miles southwest of Nacozari, arriving on January 19. At eight o'clock the next morning Pesqueira detected a cloud of dust and went in pursuit. Three hours later he overtook the Indians, who had taken a defensive position on high ground. Pesqueira and his men did not suspect that this small band was a decoy, and they charged up the slope, dislodged the Indians, and took off after them. The pursuit stopped suddenly when an estimated force of 200 warriors under Mangas Coloradas counterattacked. They swarmed around the Mexicans, who had dug in on a hillside. When night finally arrived, Pesqueira, grateful for a lull in the fighting, withdrew to a better position on another hill. Only fifteen men capable of combat remained with him. Total official casualties: twenty-six killed and forty-six wounded,[26] one of the most sweeping and decisive victories achieved by the Apaches in the nineteenth century. According to one Mexican eyewitness, the Sonorans killed or wounded seventy Apaches (probably an exaggeration).[27]

Geronimo very probably participated in this engagement. In his autobiography he speaks of a "revenge fight" in which

[42]

Ignacio Pesqueira

he was supposedly named war chief. The details are strikingly similar to contemporary reports of the battle at Pozo Hediondo. It happened, he says, east of Arizpe, and troops from Arizpe were involved. Mangas Coloradas was the leader, according to all accounts. No other fight comparable in size and significance is known to have occurred in the 1850s. Since it happened six weeks before he lost his family, he could hardly claim to have been at peace with the Mexicans or to have been seeking revenge.

From Pozo Hediondo the Apache war party withdrew to Bacoachi and on January 21 killed six citizens and captured several others—of whom three were ransomed at once.[28] On that same day Pesqueira and his survivors staggered into Cumpas, having left their dead on the battlefield. Terán y Tato assembled a fresh force of 100 men and ordered them to Pozo Hediondo to bury the dead and (he hoped) take up the trail of the Chiricahuas. Mutilated bodies and dead horses were scattered over the battle ground, and the scene of carnage so horrified the Mexicans that they refused to follow the Indians' trail.

A captured warrior from Posito's band revealed to Terán y Tato that Yrigollen had led the Chokonen in the attack on Pesqueira. This testimony was contradicted by Luis García, a native of Bacerac, Sonora, who was sent by Terán y Tato to make a complete survey of the Apache bands camped around Janos and report on their involvement in the raiding and fighting that had been going on. García believed the Janos Apaches to be innocent of any wrongdoing. The culprits, he said, were members of the Chokonen band and a group of Coyoteros from the United States.[30]

García's report to the contrary notwithstanding, Sonora's new military commander was not convinced of the innocence of the Janos Apaches. Arriving in Sonora just after the battle, Carrasco at once announced plans to avenge the defeat. After a meeting with all presidio commanders, mayors, justices of the peace, and hacienda owners of the region, he declared "a war to the death and without quarter against all tribes called Apache, excepting only the women of all ages and boys of fifteen and below."[31] He blamed the military leaders for past failures,

[44]

provoking indignant replies from González and Terán y Tato and resulting in their withdrawal from the campaign.[32]

By mid-February Carrasco had reached a decision: the Apaches at Janos must be punished, and he would do it. Toward the end of the month his expedition departed from the now-reoccupied Fronteras, headed for the Chihuahua border. On March 3 his force of 400 men crossed the boundary, unknown to the Indians and Mexicans at Janos. He was ostensibly in pursuit of seven mules recently stolen at Bacerac, some seven or eight miles south of Bavispe. This theft later proved fortunate for Carrasco, giving legitimacy to his penetration of Chihuahua.

About the time he crossed the line, Zozaya rationed 180 families at Janos. The peace commissioner had recently received two emissaries from Mangas Coloradas who expressed a wish to receive rations and live at peace in the Animas or Alamo Hueco Mountains. Four days earlier a contingent of Chokonen and Bedonkohe, under five chiefs, had arrived at Janos. Again peace was discussed but the underlying reason for their visit was to dispose of stolen Sonoran loot for whiskey and food. Whether Mangas Coloradas was present is not known; however, he had conducted business at Janos in the past so it seems quite probable that he and perhaps Geronimo were present at this time. In any event March 4 passed uneventfully at Janos despite a recent report that an invasion from Sonora was imminent. Zozaya allayed their fears, assuring the Chiricahuas that the rumor was false.[33]

Shortly after midnight on March 5, Carrasco's force was ready. He divided his troops and ordered Lieutenant-Colonel Romero to attack a rancheria situated at the Rancho de la Virgen, probably south of Janos. Carrasco, with his column, intended to approach Janos from the west and flush out any Apaches they encountered there.

Romero reached Rancho de la Virgen about 4:45 that morning and found the rancheria deserted. A trail led toward the Rancho de San Antonio, some six or seven miles east of Janos. Romero then complied with Carrasco's alternative order and marched to Janos. En route he came across seven Apaches, killed two, and captured five. By 6:30 he had reached Janos and surrounded it. A party of Apaches fled just before he arrived. Geronimo would have been with it if he were present.[34]

Meanwhile Carrasco's force had discovered and attacked Yrigollen's rancheria a few miles west of Janos. Most of the Apaches scattered and escaped upriver. Yrigollen, with three men and four women, tried to stop the attack, signalling a desire to parley, but the Sonorans killed them instantly.

Carrasco's force captured an undetermined number of Chiricahuas before reaching Janos, arriving there at seven, half an hour after Romero. He ordered Romero to take his force into Janos and seize any Apaches who had taken refuge there. It was at this point that many of the Indian casualties occurred. The Nednhi chief Arvizu,[35] Coleto Amarillo's second in command, was killed in the street. He was unarmed.

All told, Carrasco's surprise attack killed twenty-one Apaches (sixteen men and five women). Sixty-two were captured.[36]

The incident created an uproar among the Chihuahuan officials, who protested the Carrasco action on the grounds that the Apaches were residing in peace at Janos and had not raided into Sonora. The Sonorans, of course, were convinced that all the tribesmen were guilty. From the Apache point of view, the assault was perfidious and had to be avenged. From the viewpoint of officials of the State of Chihuahua, which had expended considerable money for rations in order to keep the Apaches from raiding for subsistence, the attack was an overt criminal act that seriously compromised prospects for peace.

Carrasco defended himself vigorously and held hearings at Janos, recording the testimony of captured Apaches who revealed that small raiding parties went "daily" into Sonora to rob and kill; that "every three or four moons" large war parties were organized to campaign in Sonora while their families remained in their rancherias and descended on Janos every Monday to receive their rations. On many occasions only women and children appeared for rationing. Carrasco inquired about the disposition of plunder, and the Indians confirmed what everyone in Sonora suspected: that the Apaches traded publicly in stolen mules and horses with the Janos citizens, who sold the livestock at El Paso. Finally, Carrasco claimed he recovered 300 head of stock from Yrigollen's rancheria and 38 horses from citizens of Janos. Many of these could be traced directly to Sonoran owners, and some were clearly the fruits from the Pesqueira fight, asserted Carrasco. He named five citizens of Janos as members of this alleged ring.[38]

On the morning of March 10, 1851, his investigation concluded, Carrasco left Janos with his sixty-two prisoners on his way back to Sonora. He stopped at each town on his way and received a hero's welcome with "jubilant demonstrations."[39] In Chihuahua the response was equally emotional, but for the opposite reasons. The authorities complained to Mexico City that Carrasco had crossed the state line without authorization and had attacked a camp of peaceful Indians without cause. Mexico City chose to believe Carrasco and gave him a clean bill of health.[40]

There is good reason for believing that Geronimo suffered his great loss at the hands of Carrasco's "army" (really a mixed, irregular force) of Sonorans in 1851, though the date given in his autobiography, recorded in Oklahoma in 1906 by S. M. Barrett, is 1858, one of at least four such incidents between 1844 and 1858. The 1858 fight took place at Fronteras, Sonora, while Geronimo's misfortune happened, according to his testimony, in Chihuahua, but there are better reasons for dating his tragedy 1851. The basic question which must be answered is, "When was Geronimo born?" He said he arrived in 1829, was married at seventeen, and twelve years later lost his family. By simple addition Barrett arrived at the date 1858. Geronimo's best biographer, Angie Debo, however, has shown clearly that he must have been born in the early 1820s, probably in 1823.[41] Addition then supplies the date 1851.

Other evidence supports this view. Jason Betzinez, a relative of Geronimo, also talks about the massacre which cost Geronimo his all. He locates it at Janos even mentioning that "soldiers from Sonora attacked their camp...killing many of the women and children."[42] Then there is the fact that Mangas Coloradas was involved, and even the geography, with the stream near town where the survivors gathered, is right.

The major problem with this hypothesis is the report of casualties. Carrasco claimed twenty-one killed—sixteen warriors and five women. Fifty-six of his sixty-two prisoners were women

Geronimo awaiting his fate at San Antonio, 1886.

and children. This is surprising. Usually women and children outnumbered the men in the list of the slain. It is possible, of course, that Carrasco's irregulars cut down many more women and children than Carrasco, a professional from Mexico City, cared to report. Geronimo's family may have been among the unreported dead. They may also have been among the captured and were sold into slavery. Apparently none of the sixty-two captives were ever exchanged or ransomed. Could Alope and her children have escaped death only to disappear into the interior and live out their lives as slaves?[43]

Apparently Geronimo never saw their bodies. He did not try to "recover" them, for "that was forbidden."

Over the years Geronimo has become a symbol of heroic resistance, and the massacre of his family has been cited many times to justify his transformation from a man of peace, living in harmony with nature and his neighbors, into the terror of the Southwest and northern Mexico. He was always a clamorous and persistent self-justifier, and he never admitted that he was at fault himself. His memory of the Carrasco incident was naturally selective, and he knew more than he told. The Apaches at Janos were not as peaceful as he said, and neither was he.

NOTES

[1]S. M. Barrett, *Geronimo's Story of His Life* (New York: Garrett Press, Inc., 1969), pp. 43-44.

[2]*Ibid.*, pp. 44-46.

[3]Anthropologists generally classify the Chiricahuas into three bands: Eastern (Chihenne), Central (Chokonen), and Southern (Nednhi). The Chihenne lived primarily west of the Rio Grande in southwestern New Mexico. In 1850, Mangas Coloradas, Delgadito, and Ponce were their principal leaders. The Chokonen inhabited what is today Cochise County in southeastern Arizona. Their range also extended north to the Gila and south to the Sierra Madre mountains in Mexico. Their chiefs in 1850 were Miguel Narbona, Yrigollen, and Esquinaline. Cochise assumed leadership in the mid 1850s and held it until his death in 1874. The Nednhis lived almost exclusively in northern Mexico. Coleto Amarillo, Arvizu, and Laceres led this division in the late 1840s and early 1850s.

The Chiricahuas also recalled a fourth band, known as the Bedonkohe, which was closely associated with the Chihennes in 1850. Geronimo was born into this group, which looked to Mangas Coloradas for leadership. After his death in 1863, they were apparently assimilated into the remaining three bands. Barrett, *Geronimo's Story of His Life*, pp. 12-14. Jason Betzinez, *I Fought with Geronimo* (N.Y.: Bonanza Books, 1959), pp. 14-15. Eve Ball, *Indeh, An Apache Odyssey* (Provo, Utah: Brigham Young University Press, 1980), p. 22.

[4]In the spring of 1831 Chiricahua bands living in peace near Janos, Fronteras, Bavispe, and the Santa Rita Copper Mines fled their establishments and resumed hostilities

because of a drastic curtailment in rations and increasing conflicts between citizens and Indians. Juan José Compa and Pisago Cabezón were the major ringleaders. Hubert Howe Bancroft, *History of the Northern Mexican States and Texas* (San Francisco, 1886), Vol. II, p. 596; Francisco R. Almada, *Diccionario de Historia, Geografía y Biografía Chihuahuenses* (Chihuahua, 1952), p. 38.

[5]*El Sonorense*, May 12, 1848.

[6]Archivo Historico del Estado de Sonora, Hermosillo, Sonora, Folder 199, Escalante to Governor, Fronteras, December 24, 1847, and February 10, 1848; Folder 189, Urias to Governor, January 10, 1848. Hereafter cited as AHSH.

[7]*Ibid.*, Folder 199, Arvizu to Governor, Bacoachi, March 1, 1848.

[8]*El Sonorense*, September 6, 1848.

[9]*Ibid.*, October 6, 1848.

[10]Mangas Coloradas, born in the early 1790s, dominated the Bedonkohe and Chihenne bands for nearly a quarter of a century. His influence also extended to the Chokonen, (his daughter having married Cochise) and to a lesser extent the Nednhi. He harbored a bitter enmity towards Mexicans, the result of the Johnson and Kirker massacres in 1837 and 1846. He was generally friendly until American miners whipped him at Pinos Altos, New Mexico. From this point forward he fought the Americans until he was treacherously killed by American troops in January, 1863.

[11]*El Sonorense*, January 19, 1849.

[12]AHSH, Folder 201, González to Governor, Ures, March 7, 1849.

[13]*El Sonorense*, March 21, 1849; Archivo Historico del Estado de Sonora, Arizona Historical Society, Roll 15, Cordova to Prefect de Babiacora, Banamichi, March 9, 1849. Hereafter cited as AHS. Marijenia Figueira, one of the children captured by the Apaches, was liberated by California Volunteers under Captain James H. Whitlock in early 1864. Whitlock had defeated a band of Chiricahuas near Pinos Altos, New Mexico, and recaptured Marijenia, who had been a prisoner for fifteen years. *War of the Rebellion: Official Records of the Union and Confederate Armies* (Washington: Government Printing Office, 1880-1901), Vol. 34, Pt. 1, pp. 122-123.

[14]AHS, Roll 15, Limón to González, Santa Cruz, May 1, 1849; González to Governor, Bacoachi, July 12, 1849; Aros to González, Bacoachi, May 24, 1849.

[15]*El Sonorense*, April 15, 1850.

[16]*El Sonorense*, October 6, and November 3, 1848. González was born in 1793 at Arispe. He joined the military in 1809 and rose to Captain in 1822. In 1827 he was named Adjutant Inspector for Sonora and Sinaloa. In 1836 he was instrumental in negotiating a peace with the Chiricahuas and in 1844 led a Sonoran army into Chihuahua, where he attacked "peaceful" Apaches living at Janos who, he believed, were raiding Sonora. He would retire in March, 1851, amidst controversy. Francisco R. Almada, *Diccionario de Historia, Geografía, y Biografía Sonorenses*, pp. 239-240.

[17]AHS, Roll 16, Terán y Tato to Governor, Moctezuma, March 4, 1851. José Ignacio Terán y Tato was born in the early 1800s at Bacoachi. A veteran of many Indian campaigns, he personally financed and directed many of Sonora's offensives against the Chiricahuas in the 1840s and 1850s. He died in France in 1868.

[18]AHSH, Folder 221, Commander of Santa Cruz to González, Santa Cruz, March 17, 1850.

[19]On September 9, 1849, a Chihuahuan force of thirty-seven presidio troops and sixteen citizens led by Captain Baltazar Padilla surprised an Apache camp in the Florida Mountains in southwestern New Mexico, killing twelve and capturing 19. *El Faro*, October 6, 1849.

[20]*El Faro*, July 27, 1850.

[21]The hostilities alluded to a treacherous attack led by Kirker who on July 6 and July 7, 1846, massacred 148 Chiricahuas living at peace near the presidio of San Buenaventura

in Chihuahua. Six years later Mangas Coloradas bitterly recalled the massacre: "Sometime ago my people were invited to a feast; aguardiente or whiskey was there; my people drank and became intoxicated and were lying asleep, when a party of Mexicans came in and beat out their brains with clubs." See *Conditions of the Indian: Report of the Joint Special Commission* (Washington: Government Printing Office, 1867), p. 328; *El Provisional*, July 7, 14, and 21 for primary accounts and James Kirker's Diary of Operations. George A. Ruxton described the scalps which hung over the main entrance of Chihuahua City some three months later. George A. Ruxton, *Adventures in New Mexico and the Rocky Mountains* (Glorieta, N.M.: Rio Grande Press, 1973). James Hobbs participated in the attack and reports his version, though his account is sometimes confusing and chronologically garbled. James Hobbs, *Wild Life in the Far West* (Glorieta, N.M.: Rio Grande Press, 1969), pp. 81-100. For a biography of James Kirker, see William Cochran McGaw, *Savage Scene, The Life and Times of James Kirker* (New York: Hastings House, 1972).

[22]AHS, Roll 16, Navamuelto to Governor, Magdalena, October 5, 1850; *El Sonorense*, November 15, 1850; AHSH, Folder 221, Terán Y Tato to Governor, Fronteras, November 11, 1850.

[23]The hostile Chokonen and Bedonkohe solicited peace on four occasions. Each time peace commissioner Zozaya rejected their proposals until they had first made peace with Sonora. Mangas Coloradas himself sent emissaries in January and February, 1851. Their reasons are not clear but it is likely that the lure of rations, a market to dispose of their booty, and the rumors of a Sonoran offensive influenced the hostiles to seek sanctuary at Janos. *El Correo*, April 1, 1851.

[24]*El Sonorense*, January 31, 1851. José María Carrasco was born in 1813 and reached the rank of lieutenant in 1833. He had a distinguished military career, having fought against the Americans in the Mexican War of 1846. Almada, *Diccionario de Historia, Geografía y Biografía Sonorenses*.

[25]Ignacio Pesqueira, born December 16, 1820 in Arizpe, was educated in Europe. He returned to Sonora in 1839 and joined the local military, or National Guard. By 1845 he had risen to captain and, as his biographer notes, "was suddenly catapulted from obscurity to state-wide prominence" after the Pozo Hediondo fight. He became Governor of Sonora in 1857—a position he held throughout most of the 1860s and into the 1870s. He died on January 4, 1886. Rodolfo F. Acuña, *Sonoran Strongman: Ignacio Pesqueira and His Times* (Tucson: University of Arizona Press, 1974).

[26]*El Sonorense*, January 28, 1851; *El Correo*, February 11, 1851. *El Sonorense* charged that "Anglo scoundrels" had armed and led the Apaches, who were armed with six-shooters and rifles.

Apaches killed eleven and wounded twenty-two of the fifty Nationals from Bacoachi and killed fifteen and wounded twenty-four of the fifty Nationals from Arizpe. AHSH, Folder 224, Villascusa to Governor, Arizpe, April 28, 1851.

[27]Eduardo W. Villa, *Compendio de Historia del Estado de Sonora* (Mexico: Patria Nueva, 1937), pp. 242-244. Villa errs in placing the fight on January 7.

[28]*El Sonorense*, January 31, 1851. One of the youths captured, Savero Aredia [Severo Heredia], escaped six months later to Bartlett's boundary commission. John C. Cremony, *Life Among the Apaches* (Tucson: Arizona Silhouettes, 1951), p. 60; John Russell Bartlett, *Personal Narrative of Explorations and Incidents in Texas, New Mexico, California, Sonora and Chihuahua 1850-1853* (Glorieta, N.M.: Rio Grande Press, 1965).

[29]*El Sonorense*, January 31, and February 14, 1851; AHS, Roll 16, Terán y Tato to Governor, Moctezuma, January 28, 1851. A popular version has Pesqueira's troops leaving him for dead on the battleground from where he walked to Arizpe and received a hero's welcome. Acuña, *Sonoran Strongman*, p. 16.

[30]AHS, Roll 16, Zozaya to García, Janos, February 20, 1851; AHS, Roll 16, García to Terán y Tato, Bavispe, March 1, 1851.

[31]*El Sonorense*, February 28, 1851.

[32]In defense of himself González wrote that at the time he assumed leadership in late 1848 the presidios were in a deplorable state. They were too widely separated either to impede Apaches or to take the offense. Although he concurred with Carrasco that his troops lacked discipline, he vehemently disagreed that they lacked the will or courage. The condition of the presidios had improved under his regime, González asserted. *El Sonorense*, March 21, 1851.

On March 4, 1851, Terán y Tato wrote the governor defending his actions and the honor of the National Guard. AHS, Roll 16, Terán y Tato to Governor, Moctezuma, March 4, 1851.

[33]*El Correo de Chihuahua*, April 1, 1851.

[34]*El Sonorense*, April 4, 1851.

[35]Arvizu was born in the 1790s and had lived at Janos until the outbreak in 1831. He participated in the Janos peace treaty of 1842, remaining there until January, 1844, when a smallpox epidemic drove the Apaches away. A leader in the negotiations leading to the treaty of 1850, Arvizu seems to have faithfully lived up to the peace agreements and doesn't appear to have been with the Apache parties who used Janos as a base to raid Sonora.

[36]*El Sonorense*, March 28 and April 4, 1851; *El Correo*, April 15, 1851. John Russell Bartlett and John C. Cremony both met Carrasco on May 23 when he informed them of the attack. Both reported the incidents in their accounts. Bartlett, the more accurate, reported that Carrasco killed twenty warriors and captured fifty to sixty, chiefly women and children; while Cremony, with his propensity to exaggerate, put the total Apache casualties at 130 killed and ninety captured. Dunn, in *Massacres of the Mountains*, picked up Cremony's account (p. 313). Bartlett, *Personal Narrative*, Vol. I, pp. 267-268; Cremony, *Life Among the Apaches*, p. 39. Almada, in his *Diccionario de Chihuahua*, noted that Carrasco attacked the Chiricahua band.

[37]AHSH, Folder 234, Carrasco testimony taken at Janos, March 6, 1851.

[38]One example of this occurred when a citizen from Santa Fe, José María Robles, purchased a mule from an Apache at Janos which had been stolen from Enquinos Montar, a citizen of Tepache, Sonora. The response from Janos was that Robles was just a transient passing through and was unaware of the law prohibiting trade with the Apaches, which seems to ignore the issue: How did the Apaches end up with the mule in the first place? Janos Archives, University of Texas at El Paso, Roll 33, González to Medina, Janos, May 2, 1851.

[39]*El Sonorense*, March 28, 1851. The Apache prisoners were subsequently relocated to Guaymas in early April. *El Sonorense*, April 11, 1851.

[40]*El Correo de Chihuahua*, April 29, 1851. Bartlett also reported that Carrasco had been cleared of any misconduct. Bartlett, *Personal Narrative*, Vol. I, p. 268.

[41]Angie Debo, *Geronimo: The Man, His Time, His Place* (Norman: University of Oklahoma Press, 1976), p. 7.

[42]Betzinez, *I Fought With Geronimo*, p. 17.

[43]Carrasco told Bartlett in May, 1851, that the "prisoners" were sent into the interior and there distributed among the haciendas and ranchos as servants, too far off ever to reach their homes again. Bartlett, *Personal Narrative*, Vol. I, p. 268.

CREDITS—The photograph on page 37 is from the Arizona Historical Foundation; on page 41 from the Buehman Collection of the Arizona Historical Society, Tucson; on page 43 from AHS general collections; on page 48 from the Rose Collection, Western History Collections, University of Oklahoma Library.

THE SURRENDER OF GERONIMO

by

Lieutenant Charles B. Gatewood, U. S. A.

This is Lieutenant Charles B. Gatewood's account, never published, of his part in Geronimo's surrender, transcribed from his handwritten manuscript in the Gatewood Collection, Arizona Historical Society archives, Tucson, Arizona. Casually written and hastily corrected, this account provides useful information about the last stages of the journey to Skeleton Canyon. It is specially interesting for its revelation of Gatewood's character—steadfast, honorable, and, at the same time, modest, self-deprecating, and lightened by a good sense of humor. Although he uses the language of another time (bucks, squaws, hostiles), Lieutenant Gatewood respected his Indians and they responded.

The Gatewood Collection at AHS also contains an edited version of this account by Major Charles B. Gatewood, who accumulated letters and documents supporting his father's claim to credit for the chief role in bringing about the surrender. This useful manuscript, twice as long as the original, was printed in shortened form in *Proceedings of the Annual Meeting and Dinner of the Order of Indian Wars of the United States* (Washington, 1929) and reprinted in the *Arizona Historical Review*, vol. 4 (April, 1931), pp. 33-44.

I N JULY, 1886, Gen. Miles after an interview with some of the friendly Chiricahuas at Fort Apache, A. T., determined to send two of them, Ka-teah [Kayitah] and Martin [Martine] to the hostiles with a message, demanding their surrender, promising removal to Florida or to the east. The final disposition of them was to be left to the President of the United States. I was selected to accompany them. Written authority was given me to call upon any officer commanding U. S. troops, except those of several small columns operating in Mexico, for whatever aid was needed. In his verbal instructions Gen. Miles particularly forbade my going near the hostiles with less than twenty-five soldiers escort, fearing that I might be entrapped and held as a hostage, as had been done before by other Indians.

The party was organized at Fort Bowie, in Southern Arizona, & consisted of the two Indians mentioned, George Wratten as interpreter, Frank Huston as packer, three pack mules & myself. Later on "Old Tex," a rancher, was hired as courier. The twenty-five soldiers were not taken, because a peace-commissioner would be hampered with a fighting escort in this case, & besides, that number of men deducted from the strength of the garrison at the time, would spoil the appearance of the battalion at drills & parade,—commanding officers had to give up a part of their commands.

Having all that was necessary to our health & comfort, and everybody mounted on a *good* riding mule (do you know that all mules are not good riding mules?), we set out & in three days arrived at a camp near the Mexican line, where I had been persuaded that twenty-five mounted men could easily be obtained. A company of infantry, about ten broken-down cavalry horses, & a six-mule train—and you could have knocked the commanding officer down with a feather when I showed my order and demanded my escort. However, as he had been my instructor at West Point, I took another dinner with him & didn't disturb his "mixed command," but journeyed along into Mexico. Soon after crossing the line we were escorted southward by Capt. J. Parker, 4th Cavalry, whose command consisted of a troop of cavalry and infantry detachments under Lieutenants Richardson, 8th Infantry, & Bullard, 10th Infantry. Their whole outfit didn't number more than thirty or forty men so that a deduction of the escort ordered would have put them "out of the fight." In a few days, we arrived at the camp of Captain Lawton, who has since been promoted to a Lieutenant-Colonelcy in the Inspector General's Department. Having no escort, which was my own fault, of course, for I should have taken it from Fort Bowie, I put myself under Lawton's orders, with the understanding, however, that whenever we approached the hostiles & circumstances permitted, I should be allowed to execute my

[54]

HOLBROOK / Sept. 13th - San Carlos Chiricahuas entrained

SAN CARLOS   Sept. 8th -
          Chiricahuas rounded up
      Fort Thomas

LOCATION MAP

ARIZONA

ARIZONA / NEW MEXICO

GILA RIVER

Gila River

San Pedro River

Fort Grant

A R I Z O N A
          Sept. 9th - Geronimo & party
          BOWIE   entrained
                          Southern Pacific R.R.

Santa Cruz River

Fort Lowell

TUCSON

FORT BOWIE
JULY 16th - Mission begins

Chiricahua Mtns.

Sept. 3rd - Miles arrives
Sept. 4th - Surrender

August 29th - Arrival
Skeleton Canyon
Peloncillo Mtns.

AT & SF RR

JULY 19th -
Meeting with Capt. Stretch

Fort Huachuca   CLOVERDALE
          San Bernardino   NEW MEXICO
ARIZONA   Guadalupe
SONORA   CHIHUAHUA
Nogales   Canyon
                    August 28th -
                    Arrival

August 21st -
Scouts strike trail

FRONTERAS   August 23rd -
August 20th -   Gatewood arrives
Gatewood & Lawton
arrive   Janos

                              CARRETAS
Magdalena   JULY 22nd ?

M E X I C O
                    Bavispe
Arizpe   Nacozari
                    Bacerac
          Rio Sonora   Huachinera

                    SIERRA MADRE
N   Moctezuma
SCALE IN MILES   Rio Moctezuma   Huasavas
                    Bacadehuachi
0   25   50   Nacori Chico
                    Rio Bavispe
THE LAST CAMPAIGN   August 3rd - Gatewood & Parker
GATEWOOD IN MEXICO,   arrive   LAWTON'S
July-September, 1886   CAMP

          Rio Yaqui   Rio Aros

Drawn by Don Bufkin

mission. His camp was on the Arros River well up in the Sierra Madre Mountains & perhaps two hundred and fifty miles below the boundary line. While there, news came to the effect that the hostiles were several hundred miles to the northwest, & so a movement was made in that direction. About the middle of August we learned that Geronimo's party was in the vicinity of Fronteras, Mexico, negotiating with the Mexican authorities with a view to surrendering to them. My little party with an escort of six men left Lawton's command about 2 a.m., and at night camped near Fronteras, having made about 70 miles. The next day at Fronteras it was learned that several squaws had been there with an offer of peace to the Mexicans & that Lieut. W. E. Wilder, of our army, had had some conversations with them, in regard to surrendering. The squaws had departed, going eastward with three extra ponies laden with food & mescal. The latter is a very intoxicating drink distilled from the mescal plant.

In the meantime the prefect of the district had assembled about 200 Mexican soldiers in the town, bringing them in by detachments at night, with the hope of playing the old trick of getting the Apaches drunk & then massacring the whole party. He was very much annoyed at the appearance of the American troops, but in as much as, under the treaty between the two republics, the Americans had a right to be there, he could do nothing towards getting them away, & his requests to that end availed not. He insisted that the Americans should not move in the direction the squaws had taken, because they would interfere with his well laid plans. While Lieuts. Clay, Wilder and others were trying to control the supply of wine, I took an escort of six or eight men which Wilder gave me, & Tom Horn & a Mexican as interpreters & proceeding south about six miles, struck eastward into the mountains about dark so as not to be seen by the Mexicans. Early next morning, by circling toward the north, the trail of the squaws who had been at Fronteras, was found & followed that day & the two following. Lawton was notified of what had been done, & which direction the trail was leading, by one of the escort who was to act as guide until his scouts could take up the trail. We had to march slowly &

[56]

Lieutenant Gatewood and his wife, 1882.

cautiously, with a piece of flour sack to the fore as a white flag. The country was very rough, & as we approached dangerous looking places, Artemus Ward's magnanimity—in sacrificing his relations in the war—was nothing to my desire to give Kateah & Martine a chance to reap glory several yards ahead. The trail was getting decidedly hot the third day, as it had joined that of the main body, & at the head of a cañon leading into the Bavispe valley, the two Indians halted. The cañon was uninviting, as one might say, severely unattractive, & besides, there was a pair of faded canvas pants hanging on a bush nearby. A cañon like that with such a banner at its head would make anybody halt. In the discussion of the matter, everybody gave his opinion, but nobody knew how to interpret what the pants had to say. My idea was that the two Indians should proceed several hundred yards ahead as usual, then several soldiers & George Wratten, with the pack mules & Frank Huston following, should come next, two more soldiers & myself, & a hundred yards in rear, two more soldiers. I still think that was the best plan, but the two Indians said that they were not greedy, but willing to divide the glory to be had equally among the whole party. Then everybody else agreed to go ahead with the Indians, & I volunteered too, so we all went along together. That proved to be a very innocent cañon, & I was sorry after we got through that I had not gone ahead.

A few miles further on we reached the Bavispe river where, after flowing northward, it makes a bend & turns to the south. Here we made our camp for the night in a cane brake just under a peak that commanded the surrounding country for half a mile or so. With a picket on the peak & the Indians following the trail for several miles beyond, together with the hiding places the cane brake offered in case of emergency, we felt pretty safe, though this peace commission business was getting decidedly tiresome. The white flag was high up on a century plant pole all the time, but that don't make a man bullet proof. As it turned out, Geronimo saw us all the time, but never noticed the flag, although he had good field glasses, & he wondered what fool small party was dogging his footsteps.

[58]

Taken in the fall in 1880, this photograph shows Lieutenant C. B. Gatewood of the 6th Cavalry (seated top row) with his Indian scouts. This party had pursued hostile Apaches under Victorio and Nana.

About sundown that day, Aug. 23, 1886, one of the Indians returned to us with the information that the hostiles occupied an exceedingly rocky position high up in the Torres Mountains in the bend of the Bavispe some four miles from our camp. They had both been up there & had delivered Gen. Miles' message, & Geronimo had sent one back to say that he would talk with *me* only, & that he was rather offended at our not coming straight to his *rancheria*, where peaceably inclined people were welcome. Natchez [Naiche], who was the real chief, if there was one, sent word that we would be perfectly safe so long as we behaved ourselves. Knowing that Natchez' influence was greater than any other one man among them, his message took off the keen edge of uneasiness, & besides, Lawton's scouts under Lt. R. A. Brown (30 in number) had arrived, & his command was supposed to be nearby. It being too late to visit Geronimo that day, we remained in the cane brake over night.

The next morning, with Brown's patriots, we followed the trail, feeling somewhat safer. Within a mile of the hostile camp, we met an unarmed Chiricahua who came to give us the message delivered by the Indian the day before. Then three armed warriors appeared with the suggestion from Natchez that my party & theirs should meet to discuss matters down in the bend of the river where there was plenty of wood, water, grass & shade, & also that Brown & his scouts should return to the place where we had bivouaced the night before, & that any troops that might join him must remain there. These conditions were complied with.

We adjourned to the place designated in the river bottom after passing signals (smoke & shots) signifying that all was well. By squads the hostiles came in, & unsaddled & turned out their ponies to graze, as we had done with our animals. I had on my saddle fifteen pounds of tobacco with a sufficient quantity of cigarette papers & matches, & we each carried several days rations with us,—all which tobacco & rations were put into a commissary depot with the jerked horse meat & other delicacies which the hostiles contributed. Our cook & squaw gave us several good meals.

Among the last to arrive was Geronimo. I was sitting on his brother-in-law's saddle which had been thrown on a log, &

[60]

another Indian was sitting on mine, both with the owner's arms attached. Geronimo laid his Winchester rifle down about 20 feet away & came & shook hands. He remarked my thinness & apparent bad health & asked what was the matter with me. After an answer to this question & having taken a seat alongside as close as he could get (gentle reader, turn back, take another look at his face, imagine him looking me square in the eyes & watching my every movement—twenty-four bucks sitting around fully armed, my small party scattered in their various duties incident to a peace commissioner's camp, & say if you can blame me for feeling chilly twitching movements). The tobacco had been passed around in the meantime, & everyone was puffing at his cigarette. Geronimo announced that the whole party was there to listen to Gen. Miles' message. It took but a few minutes to say, "Surrender and you will be sent to join the rest of your people in Florida, there to await the decision of the President as to your final disposition. Accept these terms or fight it out to the bitter end." They all listened attentively and a silence of several weeks fell on the party, at least so it seemed to me. Then Geronimo passed a hand across his eyes, and extending both arms forward & making his hands tremble, asked if I had anything to drink. "We have been on a three days' drunk," said he, "on the mescal the Mexicans sent us by the squaws who went to Fronteras. The Mexicans expected to play their usual trick of getting us drunk and killing us, but we have had the fun; and now I feel a little shaky. You need not fear giving me a drink of whiskey, for our spree passed off without a single fight, as you can see by looking at the men sitting in this circle, all of whom you know. Now in Fronteras there is plenty of wine & mescal, & the Mexicans and Americans are having a good time. We thought perhaps you had brought some with you." He seemed to know what was going on, but it was explained to him that we had left the town in such a hurry that we had neglected to provide ourselves with desirable drinkables. Then he proceeded to talk business. He said that they would leave the war path only on condition that they be allowed to return to the reservation, occupy the farms held by them when they left the last time, be furnished with the usual rations, clothing, farming implements, etc., with guaranteed

[61]

exemption from punishment for what they had done. If I was authorized to accede to these modest propositions, the war might be considered at an end right there. I explained that the big chief, Gen. Miles, whom they had never met, had ordered me to say just so much and no more, & that they knew it would make matters worse if I exceeded my instructions. This would probably be their last chance to surrender, & if the war continued they must all be killed eventually, or if surrendered or captured, the terms would not be as liberal. The matter was thus discussed for an hour or two, in which Geronimo narrated at length the history of their troubles, the frauds, thieving &c perpetrated by the Indian agents, and the injustices generally done them by the white people, all of which it is not necessary to relate here.

Then they withdrew to one side in the cane brake & held a private conference for an hour or so. It being about noon when their caucus adjourned, we all had something to eat with a cup of coffee. After lunch the bucks hav[ing] taken their places, Geronimo said that to expect them to give up the whole Southwest to a race of intruders was too much. They were will[ing] to cede all of it except the reservation. They would move back on that land or fight till the last one of them was dead. "Take us to the reservation or fight," was his ultimatum, as he looked me square in the eye. I couldn't take him to the reservation & I couldn't fight, neither could I run, nor yet feel comfortable. Natchez, who had taken little part in the proceedings, here said that whether they continued the war or not, my party would be safe so long as they did not begin hostilities. They came as friends, not as enemies, and [we] would be allowed to depart in peace. Knowing his influence among them, I felt considerably easier in my mind. They were then informed that the rest of their people who had remained on the reservation, between 400 and 500 in number, had been removed to Florida to join Chihuahua's band, & their going back to the reservation meant living among their enemies, the other Apaches. The mother and daughter of Natchez were among them. This put a new phase on the matter, & they had another private council. Upon re-assembling after an hour, Geronimo announced that they would continue the war, but

[62]

they wanted to "talk" all night if they could find a beef to kill to furnish the necessary meat. I objected to talking all day and all night too, but would have had to agree to it, & was much relieved to know later that no beef could be found. After considerable smoking & general conversation, Geronimo asked what kind of man the new general was. They knew Gen. Crook very well and might surrender to him. He wanted to know Gen. Miles' age, size, color of his hair & eyes, whether his voice was harsh or agreeable to listen to, whether he talked much or little, & if he meant more than he said or less. Does he look you in the eyes, or down on the ground, when he talks? Has he many friends among his people & do they generally believe what he says? Do the soldiers & officers like him? Has he had experience with other Indians? Was he cruel or kind-hearted? Would he keep his promises? In fact, his questions required a complete description of the general in every respect. They all listened intently to the answers I gave. Then Geronimo said, "He must be a good man, since the Great Father sent him from Washington, & he sent you all this distance to us."

Towards sunset, I suggested that my party repair to the camp of Lawton who had arrived that day where Brown had been sent to, about four miles down the river, & had remained there during the day at my request. That night they could discuss the matter further among themselves, & their medicine men might take a few glances into the future. To this they agreed, & Geronimo said, "We want your advice. Consider yourself one of us & not a white man. Remember all that has been said today, & as an Apache what would you advise us to do under the circumstances." It didn't take long to reply, "I would trust Gen. Miles & take him at his word." They all stood around looking very solemn, & no further reference was made to the matter, except Geronimo said he would let me know the result of their council in the morning. Before I left the camp, they wanted me to go alone, or with one man, several hundred miles across the country to the nearest American post, & communicate again with the general with a view to getting a modification of the terms. They would send a number of their warriors to protect me & warn me of any danger that threatened

[63]

Fort Bowie, Arizona Territory, in 1886, looking north.

from the Mexicans or others, tho I might not see them at all on the journey. To this I replied that it would be a useless journey, for Gen. Miles had already fully considered the matter & made up his mind. His message was final, & nothing I could say would cause him to change it. After shaking hands all around, we bade them a solemn goodbye & rode to Lawton's camp. On the way, Chappo, Geronimo's son, overtook us, & after riding a mile or so, I asked him where he was going. He replied, "With you. I'm going to sleep close to you tonight & tomorrow I'll return to camp. I have my father's permission to do so."

As the scouts & Chappo's people never had been on friendly terms, the risk of getting a knife stuck in him during the night was too great to be taken. It is easy to understand that injury to him in our camp would never do. This was explained to him, & finally he reluctantly returned to his own camp with an injunction to his noble parent why he was sent back. Sending the boy back in that way had a good effect on them as I learned afterward.

[64]

Geronimo's band leaves Fort Bowie for the train to Florida.

Arrived at Lawton's camp, I narrated to him all that had happened. The next morning, the scout pickets passed a call for "Bay-chen-daysen," my pet name, meaning "Long Nose." With the interpreter, I met our handsome friend & several of his bucks, a few hundred yards from camp. When they saw us coming, they dismounted, unsaddled their ponies, & laid their arms on their saddles, all but Geronimo who wore a large pistol under his coat in front of his left hip. After repeating the description of Gen. Miles to him, he said that the whole party, 24 bucks & 14 women & children, would meet the General at some point in the United States, talk the matter over with him, & surrender to him in person, provided the American commander would accompany them with his soldiers & protect them from Mexican & other American troops that might be met on the way. They would retain their arms until they had surrendered formally, individuals of each party should have the freedom of the other's camp, & that I should march with them & when convenient sleep in their camp. This was agreed to, & the party

[65]

entered our camp, where, upon full explanation, Lawton approved the agreement. The rest of the hostiles then moved down near us, & everybody was happy. They had very little food, & as our pack train wandered off on the wrong trail, it was a sort of starvation camp for several days, much to the amusement of the Indians. Gen. Miles was promptly informed of the situation, & Skeleton Cañon, about 60 miles south-east of Fort Bowie, A. T., was appointed the place where the general was to be met.

We broke camp Aug. 24th, & on the 26th, the disappointed Mexican commander, with about 200 Infantry, suddenly appeared from the west, & created quite a stampede among our new friends. While the command remained to parley with the Mexicans, our prospective prisoners & myself made a "run for it" northward, thro' the bushes & over the rocks, at an eight or ten mile gait. Flankers & a small advance guard were thrown out, the rear guard being composed of the bucks under Natchez. After about an hour's run, we halted so as not to be too far from the command, for in case there should be serious trouble with the Mexicans, our wards proposed to take the side of the Americans. Soon a courier arrived from Lawton informing us that the Mexican would not be satisfied until he heard from Geronimo himself that he intended to surrender to the United States authorities. An interview between the two was arranged in a new camp to be established near our present position, the Mexican force to remain several miles away. The prefect was to be accompanied by seven of his men as escort, & Geronimo by the same number, all armed. The Mexican party arrived first & were received with due formality—& hospitality. Then Geronimo at the head of his party came through the bushes, dragging his Winchester rifle by the muzzle with his left hand, & his six-shooter handy in front of his left hip. The suspicious old rascal would take no chances. As he approached I introduced him to the prefect whose name I have forgotten, & stepped back a little in rear of the latter. After shaking hands, the Mexican shoved his revolver around to his front & Geronimo drew his half way out of the holster, the whites of his eyes turning red, & a most fiendish expression on his face. The former put his hands behind him & the latter dropped his right hand by his side.

[66]

Thus serious trouble was averted. The prefect asked why he had not surrendered at Fronteras. Geronimo replied that he did not want to be murdered. Prefect: "Are you going to surrender to the Americans?" Ger: "I am, because I can trust them. Whatever happens, they will not murder me & my people." Prefect: "Then I shall go along & see that you *do* surrender." Ger: "No, you are going south & I am going north. I'll have nothing to do with you nor with any of your people." And so it was. A Mexican soldier came with us & finally returned to his country with official notice from Gen. Miles that the much dreaded Apaches had been moved to Florida.

We resumed our journey the next morning. A day or two afterward, having marched about a day's journey (15 or 20 miles), we halted & waited for the command. Hour after hour passed & no command & no rations. Lt. T. Clay, 10th Infantry, & Dr. L. Wood, U. S. A., were with us. One can of condensed milk was all we guests could muster, when the "outfit" had concluded to have something to eat & then move to a good place for our bivouac for the night. Wandering around among the people, I noticed the squaw of Periquo, brother-in-law of Geronimo, preparing a meal for the family. Thereupon I presented her with the can of milk, with a smile & a bow, & entered into conversation with him. Some venison had been obtained that morning, & with the flour, sugar & coffee, the thrifty woman had brought with her, she was cooking a toothsome repast. Periquo invited me to partake with considerable grace & dignity, &, motioning to Clay & Wood, requested their presence also. Being very hungry, we needed no second invitation. The squaw made everything clean, the edibles were well cooked, & it pleased her to see us eat so heartily. Breakfast next morning was served to us in much the same manner, though, as one of the interpreters expressed it, "Grub's getting short." The next day the command & the pack train joined us, having been piloted by a party sent out to hunt them up. A day or two afterward, at Guadalupe Cañon, considerable uneasiness was manifested by the Indians. They had killed some of Lawton's troopers at this place some months before, & Lawton was away the better part of the day. The next officer in command expressed a desire to

[67]

pitch in with the troop & have it out right there. We had stopped there, because there was no other water within 7 or 8 miles. The Indians began to mount their ponies & get out of the cañon, the squaws and children going first. Seeing Geronimo among them going up the trail, I immediately rode after him. Out of the cañon, I noticed them taking up a lively trot, & had to gallop my mule to overtake the old man. The troops having followed leisurely, we came down to a walk, & after some conversation, Geronimo asked me what I should do in case they were fired on by the troops. I replied that I would proceed toward the troops and endeavor to have the firing stopped; otherwise I would run away with them. Natchez, who had joined us, said, "You must go with us for fear some of our men might believe you treacherous & try to kill you." I cautioned them again, as had been done all along the road, to keep a good lookout all around, as there were many small columns of American troops in that region, & I must have notice of their approach so that a collision might be prevented by my going ahead & explaining matters to the officers. The Mexican troops had gotten close to us by their not keeping up their usual watchfulness. We camped a few miles further on where Lawton joined [us], & spent a rather uneasy night. It was in this camp or the next one, that several young officers proposed to kill Geronimo, during one of their talks. It was also while coming to this camp that Geronimo & Natchez proposed to me to run away from the troops, with all their people, into the mountains near Fort Bowie, & they would remain there while I went into the post to communicate with Gen. Miles & arrange for their immediate surrender to him. But I knew that the general was not at Fort Bowie, & by the time I could go there & communicate with him I feared they might be attacked & run out of the country & leave me to "hold the bag." So I advised strongly against such a proceeding. It was about this time also that I wanted to take my baggage and join some other column, stating to Lawton that I had been ordered simply to see that the two Indians went to the hostiles & delivered their message. More than that was not expected. He pointed out the necessity of my remaining, the "trouble" we would both be in if the

[68]

Rocks at Skeleton Canyon mark site of the surrender.

Indians got away, & said he would use force to keep me if
necessary. I remained.

Finally we arrived at Skeleton Cañon, where the general
came a day or two later. The Indians were generally very
anxious to meet him & Geronimo particularly lost no time in
being presented. In few words, Gen. Miles told them what he
would [do], the gist of which was that they would be sent to
Florida & there await the final action of the President of the
United States. Then to the interpreter, "Tell them I have no
more to say. I would like to talk generally with them, but we do
not understand each other's language." That settled it. Geronimo
turned to me, smiled, & said in Apache, "Good, you told the
truth." He then shook hands with the general & said he himself
was going with him, no matter what the others might do. He
followed our commander wherever he went, as if fearing he
might go away, leaving his captive behind. In the meantime,
Natchez was out in the hills several miles away, mourning for

[69]

his brother who had gone back into Mexico to get a favorite pony, & he began to fear the Mexicans had killed him. The next day, at Geronimo's suggestion, he & myself with interpreters walked over to Natchez' mourning place, to try to persuade him to come in & surrender. He had with him his own band of 12 or 15 bucks & their families, quite a large portion of the whole party. The situation was explained to him, & as the big White Chief had arrived, the presence of Natchez was necessary to complete the formalities of surrender. Among the whites such delay for the reason stated was never made, & it would appear better in him to control his grief which indeed elicited the sympathies of his white friends, & conform to the usual custom of such occasions as the present. He said that it was hard for him to do so before he learned the fate of his brother, but as he did not wish to show disrespect to the big chief, he would go immediately. He gathered his band together, brought them in, & was as much pleased with the general, as was his secretary of state, Geronimo. The next thing was to get the two Indian chiefs to agree to accompany the white chief into Fort Bowie ahead of the main body, for they were very suspicious, or had been up to that time. With a little diplomacy, this was accomplished. They made the 60 miles in one day, the rest of us taking three. From Bowie they were sent to Florida, after some delay in Texas, & finally removed to Alabama—rather suggestive as Alabama means "Here we rest."

CREDITS—The photographs on pages 57, 59, and 65 are from the Gatewood Collection of the Arizona Historical Society, Tucson; those on 64 and 69 are from AHS general collections.

A CHIRICAHUA APACHE'S ACCOUNT OF THE GERONIMO CAMPAIGN OF 1886

by

Samuel E. Kenoi

recorded by Morris E. Opler

I WAS BORN IN 1875 I remember the last time Geronimo went on the war-path. That was in 1885, but I had heard about his taking the war-path before this.

My father was a Southern Chiricahua. He ran all over the country, here, there and everywhere. He was the leader of my father's group, which was a small group. But my father did not stay with them very long. He went to San Carlos, to Fort Apache, to Mescalero. My father was never with Geronimo on the war-path.

Geronimo... was called a human tiger. He would rather be on the war-path than anything else. He would advise his parents' group, and his wife's relatives, and any other relatives, to leave and he would take them out with him. And since I have thought about Geronimo I feel this way: He was always

---

In the course of his anthropological research on the Mescalero Apache Indian Reservation in 1932, the distinguished scholar Morris E. Opler recorded the life story of Sam Kenoi, son of a Southern Chiricahua in Juh's band. While Juh's men were not followers or admirers of Geronimo, they were close to the events leading up to the surrender. Sam was sent to Florida with the other peaceful Apaches living at San Carlos. His narrative reflects the experiences of the majority of the Chiricahuas—the ones who had to suffer for the sins of a few.

Sam's account was published in the *New Mexico Historical Review*, vol. 13 (Winter, 1938), pp. 360-386, and is reproduced in part here by permission of the *Review* and its editor, Paul Andrew Hutton.

suspicious of living on the reservation as other Indians did. He was always afraid. Then there was his foolish ceremony. He thought the white people were going to kill him or send him to jail somewhere. Then he would hold his ceremony and see some vision and it would say, "Go out on the war-path."

. . . .

I know plenty of stories like this about Geronimo. Now some of the young people try to make him out a hero. They say he was a fine man and stood up and fought for his country, and things like that.

I was talking about him once at Fort Sill, and one Indian said to me, "What do you know about Geronimo?"

I said to him, "I know plenty about him. I know that he and a few others like him were the cause of the death of my mother and many of my relatives who have been pushed around the country as prisoners of war. I know we would not be in our present trouble if it was not for men like him, and you honor him for that."

I remember how it was at Fort Apache. Most of the Indians were peaceful. They were attending to business. They were raising crops. They had their sheep and cattle and were getting along very well. Then somebody would say, "Geronimo is out again," and there he would be with a small band of about forty men up in the mountains. Pretty soon he would raid a settlement here, or kill a person, and the whole tribe would be blamed for it. Instead of coming and getting his rations and settling down and trying to be civilized, he would be out there like a wild animal, killing and raiding. Then they would organize the Chiricahua scouts and send them out after Geronimo's men. In this way he caused Apache to fight Apache and all sorts of trouble to break out among our people.

. . . .

In 1885 Geronimo went on the war-path again. Some of those who stayed on the reservation were sympathetic toward Geronimo because they didn't know any better. General Nelson A. Miles, General Lawton (Captain Lawton at that time),

Sam Kenoi and his grandson playing Indian at Mescalero.

Captain Crawford, 1st Lieutenant Gatewood, 2nd Lieutenant Britton Davis, were all at Fort Apache.

Uncus'[1] father, George Noche, was called by General Miles one night. General Miles said, "I want you to organize the Chiricahua Apache Scouts to run down the renegades."

And I feel that General Miles did the right thing to organize Apache scouts who knew the country in Arizona, New Mexico, and Old Mexico. These Indian scouts were familiar with all the water holes, with all the rough country, and all the trails in that region. George Noche was highly respected by General Miles. Whenever General Miles wished to do anything about the bandits, he asked George Noche.

After the troop was organized, they gave them two rounds of ammunition and issued them Springfield U. S. Army rifles. The only thing they issued them in the way of clothing was a coat, a black uniform coat. To show who was a non-commissioned man and who was not, they wore their coats. Those non-commissioned wore their stripes according to what they were. And they made George Noche sergeant major. They claim George Noche knew all the country. He was not a leading man among the Indians, however.

Another night George Noche was called again. That night General Miles told Noche, "I'm going to give you two days and two nights. I leave it to you to decide which is the best way to get Geronimo and his band. I have sat here day and night and I have tried my best with white troops to catch Geronimo, but all my attempts seem to have failed. Now I give you two days and two nights to think about it, and on the morning of the second day you come back and let me know. That's why I called you over here." That's what General Miles told George Noche.

So George Noche told General Miles, "There is no need for you to give me two days and nights to think it over. It seems to me right now I know how to get that man. I appreciate and thank you for the high respect you show to me to do this important work. Now I want to tell my plan to get that man. If it doesn't work you can get someone else. It's the best I can do. If you agree to it we can set out tomorrow.

"Here's my plan. I have two men here for you, Kaitah and Martine. I will have a talk with them in the morning and bring them over to you. I will tell you the reason I have chosen these men. Martine has many close relatives in that band and so has Kaitah. Also Geronimo is Kaitah's relative-in-law. So it would be almost impossible for those bandits to kill these men. It is impossible to send any other men, for they will not come back alive."

General Miles was well pleased with Noche's idea. He said, "We must do that."

George Noche saw Martine and Kaitah. In the morning they went to General Miles with George Noche. They agreed to it. He enlisted them as scouts, issued them guns and gave them each a mule. So they went out the following day, starting for Mexico. They told General Miles that when they got Geronimo they would bring him to Fort Bowie, Arizona.

Those men went by themselves with Lieutenant Gatewood of the 6th Cavalry. In a day or so the 3rd Cavalry with a hundred Indian scouts set out for Mexico too, to look for him. And in the meantime Mexican soldiers ran Geronimo into Arizona; then these soldiers chased him into Mexico again. They were hot on his trail.

• • • •

Apache scouts at work tracking. Black coats were their uniforms.

Meanwhile Kaitah, Martine, George Wratten, and Gatewood were out. All the troops and Indian scouts were looking in different parts of the country for Geronimo. And Kaitah and his bunch were trailing them too. A body of troops was following Kaitah and the others, many miles behind.

They came to a mountain called Sierra Madre. They were down at the foot of the mountain, and they saw those men at the top of the mountain. While they were down on the flat, Kaitah hoisted up a white flag to them. Kaitah says Martine was afraid to go up. Martine must have been behind him, always tying his shoestring or something. Kaitah told the two white men to stay down, and he started up with the white flag. Martine wasn't anywhere in sight.[2]

[75]

Geronimo's men were pretty well armed and ready. Before Geronimo knew it was Kaitah he ordered his men not to let any man get up to that place or down alive.

Kaitah kept on going up till he got in sight, and they knew it was Kaitah. He stopped once in a while, for he thought they were going to shoot at him.

After they were sure it was Kaitah, his relatives said, "Come on up. No one is going to hurt you."

Then he went up there. He sat up there and talked with all those men. Still Martine hadn't come in sight.

Kaitah told these men, "All of you are my friends, and some of you are my brothers-in-law. I think a lot of you Indians, and I don't want you to get killed. The troops are coming after you from all directions, from all over the United States. You people have no chance whatever. The War Department's aim is to kill every one of you if it takes fifty years to hunt you down. But if you people come as the government wants you to do, they will not harm you at all. Everything is against you. Even pieces of stick will hurt you. At night you do not rest as you should. If you are awake at night and a rock rolls down the mountain or a stick breaks, you will be running. The high cliff even is your enemy. At night you go around, and you might fall off the cliff. You have the wild animals for your enemies. You even eat your meals running. You have no friends whatever in the world.

"So I beg you, my friends, do what the government wants you to do. That's what I'm up here for. I have followed you people around for several months. It's not a very pleasant life. So agree with me. I live at the agency. I live peaceably. Nobody bothers me. I sleep well; I get plenty to eat. I go wherever I want, talk to good people. I go to bed whenever I want and get all my sleep. I have nobody to fear. I have my little patch of corn. I'm trying to do what the white people want me to do. And there's no reason why you people shouldn't do it. I'm doing it. I know you people could do it. You all agree with me and behave yourself and go back to the reservation with me. We'll live longer, more happily, and rest better. So I want you to go down with me when the troops come, and they want you to come down on the flats and have a council with them."

[76]

Apache stronghold—campground in the Sierra el Tigre, Chihuahua, Mexico.

Apache gateway—where the Bavispe River leaves the mountains.

Then all these men said, "All right, we'll do what you say, and we'll come down."

Kaitah had kept watching for Martine. Martine hadn't come up yet all through the conversation. And Kaitah wondered what was wrong, and he went down a little way. There was Martine coming, listening for gun-fire too, I guess. And when Kaitah came to Martine he ordered him to go down and tell Wratten to run his horse back and get those troops on the flat as fast as possible. So Martine went.

When he came back Kaitah was eating and joking with the men. Then the troops came. They came where Lieutenant Gatewood was. So at that time they sent a despatch to Fort Bowie that they had Geronimo and that General Miles should meet them half way. Then they brought all those families down.

They had a little talk. They came to an agreement to take them to Fort Bowie. Right here one army officer told them that General Miles would meet them on the way to Fort Bowie. They hadn't disarmed them yet. That day they took them and went with them all day till dark. They weren't guarded. Some of those men were running on the side, hunting as they went along. Next day General Miles met them. He came in a government stage coach. They met again the next day.

General Miles, when he met them, asked Geronimo to hold a conference with him. General Miles, the way Kaitah tells this story, said, "The people of these three states, the State of Arizona, the State of New Mexico,[3] and the State of Mexico, are enforcing laws to capture you or bring you back dead. We were forced to look for you. When we are forced to look for you, we must carry out our orders. We are like slaves. We have to do according to what the people of the United States say. In these two states, New Mexico and Arizona, the governments and the people do not like the way you have been treating them, killing them, taking their stock and destroying the homes of the settlers. They made a law to force the War Department either to kill you or bring you back alive. If you fight, we will kill you. If you surrender, we will bring you back alive. You have killed many settlers, killed many soldiers, and taken their horses and mules and other equipment. The people do not like it. You see

[78]

Young Apaches ready for war, early 1880s.

those mountains over there. If you do not agree with me that what I am telling you is the best thing you could do, I give you the privilege to go to your mountains. I'll give you a whole night and a day before I follow your gang. Then I shall kill every last one of you, even your children. But if you want to go back with me to Fort Bowie and be peaceful and faithful like other Apaches who are at Fort Bowie and San Carlos, all right. Take your choice.

"The government has spent several million dollars in order to catch you. You have taken many lives. You have destroyed many homes. Those people you have destroyed are human just like you. They wanted to live. Why should you do that? And there's Kaedine.[4] He was one of the dangerous young war chieftains. He's right here in the midst of us now. He has rendered me a great service. A two year sentence in a California Federal prison has done him good. Since he got back he admits that he used to do wrong. I have high respect for him, for turning into as good a man as he is since he got back.

"Now, Geronimo, Naiche, all you men, members of this band, you could do as well as this Kaedine did, maybe better. Instead of that you have everything on earth against you, and you live, dodging people, like a coyote, ambushing innocent people. I'm here under authority to take you to Fort Bowie. There I will put you in prison until further orders from Washington. Now I'd like to hear from you," he told Geronimo.

Now Geronimo talked. He didn't say very much. What little he said covered a lot though.

"I agree with you about taking us back. You said just the right thing when you told me that everything is my enemy. It's just the way of you white people. You always have a ground of your own to make your statement as though it was the only true statement. But there is still something that causes you to criticize us in that manner. The earth is listening to us. The winds listen to us. The sun sees us and hears everything we say, all these things.

"The second time I went on the war-path it was because of your having so many Indian secret service men telling you some false story about me. 'Geronimo is going to do this,'

[80]

General Nelson A. Miles

'Geronimo says this,' 'You ought to have Geronimo in some jail,' and so on. Some of your own white soldiers, when they saw me and some of my men, would motion as though they were going to cut our throats.

"When I was on the reservation before, you people taught me nothing. You did not come to my home or teach me how other people live. You are here right in the midst of these soldiers. Where have you ever tried to help me? Then you criticize me for killing white people here. I did kill many Mexicans, but I have never killed as many white people as you say I have. I know some of your big generals. You become generals just because you are good liars. Why I tell you that you are a liar right in the midst of your troops is that you never have caught me shooting. And now, General Miles, I have come with my men to you with good will, but I know just what you are going to do. You will say this, I know: 'I have caught Geronimo while he was shooting and made him surrender to me.'" That's what he told General Miles.

"I'm here. The earth, the sun, and the winds all listen to me. Yusn[5] listens to me. I do not lie to you. I lay my arms down. I will not ask for mercy. If you wish, line us up and shoot us today or tomorrow. I won't care. I'll take my medicine like a man. So here's my gun." And he and his men laid their guns down.

Then General Miles talked again. He shook hands with Geronimo. "No, don't have that idea, Geronimo. We do not kill people who don't offer any fight. What I said a while ago to you, I repeat. I will take you back to Fort Bowie, have you under guard as prisoner until further orders from Washington. As I said a moment ago, I have to carry out my orders from the War Department." And General Miles said, "I myself do not like the idea, but I'm a soldier of the United States, and I get my orders. If I don't obey them, they have me under guard just as I'm going to have you under guard. Don't worry about what they may do to you, for you are causing all this trouble; you brought it on yourself."

So they took all their arms. Then they decided to go. They took Geronimo in that coach, and Naiche and Perico and the

[82]

principal men rode with Miles. The men, women, and children were followed by Indian scouts and several troops of cavalry. In a day or so they were in Fort Bowie. They had Geronimo already under guard in prison when the rest got there. They had that small band in prison, women, children, and all. They had those men and women under armed guard, had them working with picks and shovels making ditches around the post. They had Chihuahua's little band, just a few men, already in prison when Geronimo arrived. They were working too, under armed guard.

And Mangus was still out with a very small group, three or four men. General Miles had spoken at the council with Geronimo about this and told Geronimo, "It is not necessary to run down Mangus, because it will mean just so much more expense, more hardships for the soldiers. He can keep going if he wants to, but he will not get anywhere; for I know, Geronimo, when he hears that you and Chihuahua have made peace with the government, he will not be out there by himself any longer. I know he will come into one of these reservations, San Carlos or Fort Apache."

That first band captured in the fall of 1886, Chihuahua's little band, they took to Fort Marion, St. Augustine, Florida, and put them in prison.[6] It's one of the oldest posts in the United States, right on the edge of the ocean, where, when the heavy tide comes in, it flaps against the building. It is an old Spanish fort made of stone and cement.

Geronimo's band, the second group captured, was taken to San Antonio, Texas. They had them in prison there for several months.

The third group taken was composed of the faithful Indians who lived at Fort Apache. After all the Indian scouts came home from the expedition, when they thought they were all at home at Fort Apache, they called all the Indian scouts together and lined them up.[7] Then the commander ordered his troops to take their belts and ammunition and their guns away from them. By order of the commander to his soldiers, they herded the scouts in the horse barn and guarded them day and night. They threw them horse blankets to lie on. Soldiers guarded them, the very men they had gone out with before. If they wanted to urinate, the soldiers went with them.

After these Indians had gone through all these hardships for the good of the people of these two states, they did this to them. Many of these scouts and most of the other Indians were farming all this time at the agency. Some of them had sheep, some had goats, some had mule teams, wagons, harnesses; some of them had horses and fine saddles.

The Chiricahua scouts did not know what was happening. That night the Western Apache gave a big social dance, and the women were in there dancing. No one was worried. Suddenly the escort wagons were there. They herded the children, the women, and the old men at the camps down to the agency. They loaded them on escort wagons. They wouldn't allow any of them to carry any kind of weapon. They just let them take what they had on, a shawl, a blanket. All the crops were ready to be gathered. I was about ten or eleven years old then, and I was one of them.

The nearest railroad station was at Holbrook, Arizona. It is about a hundred miles away, maybe a little more, I don't know. That's where they were taking us, to load us on a train for Fort Marion, St. Augustine, Florida, the same place where Chihuahua was. They took us from Fort Apache to Holbrook in escort wagons, a two or three days' trip in escort wagons, strung out, a long way.

I was with my father in an escort wagon. My mother was with some other people. I didn't know where she was until we got off at Holbrook. Then I found her. At Holbrook the Indians had a big dance that night with the Western Apache scouts, Negroes, and white people all present.

We didn't know where we were to be taken from Holbrook. Some thought we were going to be taken to the ocean and thrown in. Some thought we were going to be killed in some other way.

These people, these Chiricahua Apache, who lived at Fort Apache peacefully, and the scouts who had helped the army run down Geronimo's band, were taken to prison for what Geronimo had done.

Above, Kaitah (left) and Martine, the Apache scouts who took Gatewood to Geronimo, at Mescalero about 1905. Below, captive Apaches at San Antonio in 1886 include the faithful Martine (third from right).

[85]

And I say this much about it. The white man plants corn. But he puts two kernels in the ground. One good kernel will yield, but one rotten kernel will kill the good one if you put them together. So, as smart as the white people pretend to be, there's one time they planted a good kernel with a rotten one. The shadow of the shameful way they treated these faithful Indians and United States Scouts still lies over us.

At Holbrook, Arizona, they loaded us on a train, and they took us to Fort Marion, St. Augustine, Florida.

It was the first time most of us had seen a train. When that train was coming along the river and it whistled, many said it was run by lightning, and they began to pray to the train. I saw many old men and women doing this. They said, "Bless us, that we may be blessed wherever we go."

Lots of the children were running out in the brush. They were afraid of the train. The soldiers had to chase them and get them in. I ran away from them; they had to catch me. I was afraid. I was thinking that they were taking me somewhere to kill me. I was so afraid. I had so much serious fear in me, that I don't know how I felt.

It took us about a week to get to St. Augustine. There were two soldiers at each door. The train stopped somewhere around Albuquerque, New Mexico, in the plains, and we were told to get off. The Chiricahua all thought it was their last day. The soldiers came with hardtack barrels and fed us. The rest of the time we ate on the train. They drove us back in there and we went on. It was the only time we got off. The soldiers kept making motions as if they were going to cut our throats every time they went through the train to give coffee. The Indians, poor and ignorant, took it that they were going to have their throats cut.

There was one scout, Massi, who jumped off the train.[8] He jumped in a sandy place somewhere in Colorado. He got away. He was one of the scouts who had been in that battle where Crawford had been killed. He's a relative of Stephen, Duncan, and Benjamin.[9] He was related to Duncan's father. He got back here and was wild for a long time. He never came to town. Once he ran away with a woman who was gathering piñon nuts at Rinconada. He forced her to go. He just threw her on his back and went off to the San Andreas Mountains. They chased him but couldn't catch him.

This woman is still living and is the wife of a Spanish-American.[10] She told the story once that he sent her home with all the children. She came back with a lot of children. All died except one, who is living now. She's married to a Mescalero. Those children were born in the wilds. This woman was a Mescalero. She's a relative of Marion Simms,[11] calls him cousin.

On that train we slept the best we could sitting up. Little children were put in that rack where you put packages.

We arrived, the last party, in that place at night, moonlight, about ten or eleven o'clock. It's a big place made out of cement and stones. It has a great dungeon under it. It's dark; even in daytime you have to carry a lantern. Those dungeons are filled with nothing but cannon balls and ammunition. There is a big place about fifteen yards wide all around on top, with a cement wall about four feet high so you couldn't fall over. On each corner of that wall is a square, a little tower made out of stone and concrete with windows on each side. It was a lookout tower, I believe. On that run-around they had been setting up army tents thick. We were up there on a cement floor, and we had no privilege to move our tents. We had to stay right there.

And they had a big gate down there where they brought us in, and it was guarded by soldiers. The Indians were not allowed to leave that gate without permission. Just certain people were allowed to get out.

They began to send the children to schools, the ones about fourteen or fifteen years old who were able to go. In the morning they strung out those poor children, and without trying to dress them up like their own class of people, they sent them to school. Wearing moccasins, some of them, some of them going barefooted, they were compelled to go to the Catholic school in the city. They wore their loin cloths, wore rags around their heads, and were bare-legged. And they sent them into that city to the Catholic school every day until the Catholic school was burned down one night. These Chiricahua children were turned in as prisoners every evening. They were watched as well as the older people.

Later General R. H. Pratt (Captain Pratt then) was selected

[87]

Geronimo (left), Naiche, and Mangus at Fort Pickens, 1887.

as Superintendent of Carlisle Indian School in Pennsylvania. He came to Fort Marion, took all the children under the authority of the Department, put them on board ship to New York somewhere. From there they took a train to Carlisle Indian School. Some of those children who were taken from there are still living today—Duncan Balachu, Arnold Kinzuni, Charlie Isti, Dora Isti, Hugh Chee, Asa Dat-ogi, David Kaja, and others. There were over a hundred children taken. The ones that went to Carlisle were only at St. Augustine one month.

I have told you that Chihuahua was the first, and the biggest bunch, the faithful tribe, came next. I don't know how many months we were there when Geronimo and his band came. They shipped him right to an island, to Pensacola, Fort Pickens. We could see the island from Fort Marion.

We were at Fort Marion for about six months. At Fort Marion my mother, my sister, and I lived in one of those tents.

[88]

They issued out bread and meat each day. We did our own cooking. There was no wood there. Wood was given, a little, and a place to cook was provided in one of the dungeons below. We had to sleep on the hard cement floor. It was warm there in Florida. Bananas grow there.

It was a tough life. I was a little fellow, and I never stole anything, never did harm to anyone. They kept me a prisoner for twenty-seven years. It's the same with Blind Tom.[12] He was blind; he wasn't harming anyone, but he was taken prisoner too. He had to be led around. If I were offered a hundred more years of life like that, I would say "No." Many died at St. Augustine. We were not used to the climate.

As I told you, the worst bandits, Geronimo and his people, they put on the island over there, Pensacola. Geronimo, Naiche, Perico, Jasper Kanseah,[13] Jewett Tisnoltos, and Asa were there. Chihuahua was not there then. He had been out with Geronimo on the war-path from the beginning, but when things got too hot, they separated from Geronimo's band and got chased to Fort Bowie, Arizona. This was in 1886. They were the first ones to be sent away. They were sent to Florida—Chihuahua, Ozoni, his brother, Eugene, Ramona, Hosea Second, and others. They were all relatives it seems. The women were sent too, whole families. This was about a month before Geronimo was captured.

Kaitah and Martine were taken with Geronimo's people. They had gone up to the Sierra Madre to get Geronimo to surrender. They had done a valuable service to the government. Still they were taken prisoner. They took them to San Antonio, Texas. They had them in prison there for about a month or so. And all those scouts who had been after Geronimo were straying back to Fort Apache. Some got in in a week; some took longer. They came in on foot, with sore feet, and some nearly starved. Then they were made prisoners.

Geronimo's band was taken to Fort Pickens, Pensacola, an island near the shore where we were. We knew they were there because when the army ship went from the shore to the island some men went along and saw them. But they didn't come over and visit us. They were not allowed to leave. The women of that band were there too, whole families were there.

[89]

[1]Uncus, a blind Chiricahua now past middle age, was alive and was employed as agency interpreter at Mescalero when this story was being recorded.

[2]There has been some dispute between the Martine and Kaitah factions concerning the bravery of Martine on this occasion. Certain it is that Kaitah was more closely related to members of Geronimo's band and therefore stood in least danger. Both Kaitah and Martine acted as informants for me during my ethnological field-work. Kaitah has since died, but Martine was alive in 1935 and may still be living.

[3]Both Arizona and New Mexico were still territories at this time, of course.

[4]The name means "No Arrows" and implies that the individual is so brave he has shot them all. Kaedine was one of the leading spirits of the Chiricahua raids of the early '80s. After his surrender to General Crook in 1883 the prison sentence to which reference is made was imposed. After his return he assisted the government in pacifying the rest of his tribesmen.

[5]Yusn is an Apache loan word from the Spanish Dios. The final n is a relative, having the force of "he who is."

[6]Chihuahua has a son, Eugene Chihuahua, and a daughter still living at Mescalero.

[7]The Indian scouts referred to are the Chiricahua who had been serving the government in the Geronimo campaign.

[8]This individual has been confused with Apache Kid and is often spoken of as the Apache Kid by white men who live in the vicinity of the Mescalero Indian Reservation.

[9]Stephen Gaji, Duncan Balachu, and Benjamin Astoyah are the persons meant. So far as I know, the first two are still alive at Mescalero. The last named has died recently.

[10]This woman has since died.

[11]Marion Simms, a prominent Mescalero Apache, has died since this account was taken.

[12]Blind Tom Lasinasti was still living at Mescalero recently.

[13]Jasper Kanseah was chief of police at Mescalero when this account was being recorded.

CREDITS—The photograph on page 73 is reproduced courtesy of Lynda Sanchez; the photographs on pages 75, 81, 85 (bottom), and 88 are from the general collections of the Arizona Historical Society, Tucson; on pages 79 and 85 (top) from the Gatewood Collection, AHS; on page 77 from Richard D. Fisher, Tucson.

GEORGE WRATTEN
FRIEND OF THE APACHES

by
Albert E. Wratten

G EORGE MEDHURST WRATTEN saw his first Apaches in 1879 when he was fourteen years old. He had come with his family from Sonoma, California, to Florence, Arizona, in that year. His father, who practiced law and owned a vineyard, had suffered business reverses, was in failing health, and hoped to make a new start in a new location. George soon became restless in his new home, however, feeling that there was nothing for him to do there and no chance of getting an interesting job. He obtained permission from his father, along with a five-dollar gold piece, to go over to nearby Globe to live with his sister Edith, who was working in a saloon and dance hall there.

The Apaches had been concentrated on the San Carlos Reservation near Globe, supervised by the military, and when a job turned up on the post, George took it. In a letter dated April 15, 1955, Jason Betzinez (author, with W. S. Nye, of *I Fought with Geronimo*) had this to say about how it happened:

Albert E. Wratten (1906-1979) was born on the Apache Indian Reservation near Fort Sill, Oklahoma, the youngest of five children. He spent his active years with the U.S. Postal Service, but his absorbing interest was in the career of his father, George M. Wratten, who devoted thirty-eight of his forty-seven years to the Apaches as government scout and interpreter, superintendent on three reservations, and persistent defender of their rights and interests. He never asked for or received any official recognition, and his son hoped to bring him the appreciation he deserved by printing his life story. He put together a 700-page manuscript but never found a publisher. This essay, assembled from Albert's collection at the Arizona Historical Society, covers the essential facts of George's career. Albert made note of his sources but felt that footnotes were pedantic. The editor has added documentation.

I have known George Wratten ever since he was sixteen years old. He ran away from his home in Florence, Arizona, and came to San Carlos with a party of people who built a general store and young Wratten was one of the clerks in the store, where he was in daily contact with the Indians constantly, and soon learned their language. The Apache Indian language is the hardest to learn but the young Wratten exceptionally learned and understood the language in such short time and as far as we know there isn't another white man could speak the Apache language as freely as George M. Wratten.

He must have had a great capacity for learning, for the Chiricahua, Warm Springs and White Mountain Apaches on the reservation spoke different dialects. He learned all three by swapping information and learning new words when the Apaches came into the trading post to make their purchases. Rogers Toclanny declared in a conversation which took place at Mescalero on July 4, 1959, "Your father spoke our Apache dialects better than any white man I ever knew." Through Rogers and the friendship of many others, Wratten was adopted into the Apache tribe, became a blood brother to Rogers, and resolved to dedicate his life to the welfare of the Indians.

The bad situation at San Carlos had aroused George's sympathy and interest. The reservation was a wilderness area of some 4400 square miles controlled by the Agency from its headquarters on forty acres just north of the confluence of two rivers, the Gila and the San Carlos. Jason Betzinez described it as he remembered it in the 1880s:

The Agency consisted of a few adobe buildings situated on the gravelly flat between the two streams, with a few scraggly cottonwoods offering the only shade in a place where the temperature often reached 110 degrees or higher. Dust storms were common the year round and in all seasons except the summer the locality swarmed with flies, mosquitoes, gnats, and other pesky insects. The place was almost uninhabitable, but we had to stay there. The only source of contentment that we had was that we were untroubled by the attacks of enemies, and the government did feed us after a fashion. Quite a bit of strong language, both in official reports and in later reminiscences, has been used by Army officers concerning the way we were cheated out of our rations by unscrupulous or careless agents.

[92]

Indian trading stores, San Carlos Reservation, 1880.

Apaches crossing the Gila River at San Carlos.

Thanks to his job in the Post store, George saw clearly how the system worked. He noted that the agents sent to San Carlos were lazy and that they made no attempt to make friends with the Indians. Some of them were crooked and stole the Apaches' food. Just staying alive was often a problem for those poor people. Jason's account continues:

We were issued rations once a week and as we were not allowed to wander away to hunt game, we were entirely dependent on this issue. The Agency was across the river from us. Since our ration would be given to someone else if we were not present at the issue, we had to get there even when the water was high. Our method of crossing under such circumstances was to make cottonwood rafts and have a swimmer pull these across by tow ropes clenched in his teeth.

George's older sister Edith, interviewed at her home in Oakland, California, in 1940, said that George was the only one able to swim the river. On issue day he was sometimes kept very busy.

It can be imagined what this situation did to a boy of fifteen or sixteen who was in constant contact with the Apaches, was learning all about them, and was beginning to understand that they were badly mistreated human beings. He soon became somewhat of a buffer between them and the officials in control — the officers and agents.

His close ties with the Indians and his ability to communicate with them brought about a great change in his life in 1881. Only sixteen years old, he became a Chief of Scouts for the U.S. Army.

He was mature for his age and had already reached his full height—five feet ten—with a well-muscled, athletic body. Quiet and reserved in manner, he had a pleasant face and silvery-gray hair down to his shoulders.[1] It was no miracle that he was given the job. He was reported as Chief of Scouts under Lieutenant C. M. Schaeffer, Quartermaster, at Fort Stanton, New Mexico, at a salary of $100 per month on October 1, 1881. On July 1, 1882, he was transferred to Fort Cummings, New Mexico, reporting to Lieutenant J. B. Goe, Quartermaster, and on October 1, 1881, he was moved to Fort Bowie, Arizona,

[94]

George Wratten in his prime, ready to inspect work at Fort Sill.

under Lieutenant J. M. Neall, as Superintendent of Trains.[2] This was an important advancement, for General George Crook was effectively supplying his troops in the field by pack train. As General Hugh L. Scott says, Crook was "the father of the modern aparejo train."[3]

George's movements during this period cannot be followed in detail, but when Geronimo made his final break-out from San Carlos in 1885, Wratten was in the field with the scouts and pack trains. Lieutenant Wirt Davis's "Itinerary" of his foray into Mexico late in 1885 lists George as Chief of Scouts with the fifty men in Company B of the 9th Cavalry.[4] He was not with Crook on March 29, 1886, when Geronimo came in for the meeting at Canyon de los Embudos near the border—at least his name is not mentioned—and he was on leave, visiting friends in Albuquerque, when Geronimo made his final break on May 17. In July Wratten was back in harness, entering the final stages of the campaign in which he was to play such an important part. He told about it in the only interview he is known to have given, an informal conversation conducted during a visit to Washington in 1905 when Geronimo was a featured participant in President Theodore Roosevelt's second inaugural parade. Wratten accompanied him as mentor and guardian and talked at length at headquarters in the Capitol Hotel with Dr. S. M. Huddleson, a niece of Charles B. Gatewood. She gave her account, probably not quoting George word for word, to Gatewood's son Charles in 1925.[5] After some general conversation, Wratten got to the point:

I met Lieutenant Gatewood in Albuquerque, N. M., one day and he told me he was making up a party to go and get Geronimo to give up. He said that Geronimo and his band were into much devilment across the border in Mexico and that he believed he knew where Geronimo could be found. He asked me to go along with him on the hunt. We got ready and started from Fort Bowie, Arizona.

No! We weren't *afraid*! We had many such ugly jobs to do in the earlier days and never thought very much of them. I could tell you of several dozen more blood-curdling incidents in our lives than the so-called capture of Geronimo. It has been so long ago now that I am a bit hazy as to exactly how many others went along with us, but I think that towards the last there were eight of us all told, including some soldiers that joined down in Old Mexico. There were, of course, Lieutenant Gatewood, his two Indian scouts, and myself, and perhaps three or four white men .... Gatewood was taking the hostile Indians a message from General Miles asking them to surrender. Yes, they were given certain promises in order to induce them to surrender—their lives were to be spared and the Government would get them out of Arizona before the civil authorities could arrest them and try them for murder. They were to go with their families to Florida and maybe after a while could come back to Arizona when things quieted down, say in two years or so.

They traveled for a week, Wratten went on, living on cracked corn and molasses, and finally, after crossing the Bavispe River, located Geronimo and his men looking down at them from a vantage point high in the mountains. Gatewood hoped they were waiting for a conference, but he couldn't be sure.

We lay on our rifles all night, just to be ready in case of need, for we had not yet had our talk with them, and didn't know just what they would do. At sunrise we went up the mountain under a flag of truce. Some of the warriors met us before we had gone very far, and asked that we meet Geronimo and Natchez down by the river bank. We went there and hadn't been in camp for more than eight minutes before the whole blood-thirsty band began pouring in from the bush.

Well—yes—we did begin to feel a *little* creepy when we saw we were badly outnumbered and surrounded. There were about thirty-five or forty hostiles around us before the pow-pow started, and I began to feel as though there might just as well have been three or four hundred. There were only three or four white men in our party. Lieutenant Gatewood entered the camp first, and when Geronimo came, he gave the rest permission to come too.

The first thing the Indians asked for was tobacco and liquor. No liquor was available, of course, and very little tobacco, but Gatewood managed to locate some and have it brought in with a little food. Then the negotiations began and Geronimo said he was willing to surrender. George was interpreting and knew exactly what Geronimo said.

Would you believe me?—old Geronimo told Gatewood, "I am your friend and I'll go with you anywhere." He always had great faith in Lieutenant Gatewood, for he had never deceived him. He was the only man who could safely have gotten within gun-shot of the old savage, and General Miles knew that when he sent him out. Certainly the Indians knew who we were all the time. They would have picked us off long ago if they hadn't [known] while we were following them and trying to catch up.[6]

Wratten as interpreter played a vital part in the proceedings. Next to Gatewood, he was the white man the Indians trusted most. They depended on Gatewood and Wratten and would have nothing to do with other Army men.

The "long, hot, dusty trail" led to Skeleton Canyon on the border, where General Miles accepted Geronimo's surrender and made promises he did not keep. He sent Geronimo and Naiche on to Fort Bowie in a wagon, with Wratten included as interpreter. On September 8, 1886, the Apaches were on their way to Florida, expecting to be reunited with their families, who had been captured previously and were already in custody at Fort Marion. In addition to the thirty-eight members of Geronimo's group, some sixty other "undesirables" were added. With guards, scouts and officers, the party filled five special cars.[7] George Wratten traveled with them. Captain Henry W. Lawton may have asked for him, or he may have volunteered. In either case he went willingly.

After two days' travel the party reached San Antonio and were quartered in tents at the San Antonio Barracks (Fort Sam Houston), then under construction. The *San Antonio Express* reported that "George Wratten interpreted for the Chiricahuas and troopers alike."[8]

The post was immediately invaded by a mob of curious people wanting to see the captives, making things difficult for the Indians and for their guards. At the same time the newspapers, according to Dept. Commander General D. S. Stanley, were protesting against the supposed pampering of the prisoners. They "have been taken around in carriages to see the sights and have even been conducted into the Lone Star Brewery there." Although Captain Lawton and his soldiers were "barely noticed,"

Bowie Station, 1886. Accompanying the Apaches to Florida was George Wratten, seated on the ground, top row, in a light hat.

Geronimo was "the recipient of bouquets, the children supplied with candy, and the squaws with ribbons, money, etc., by the best ladies of the city."[9]

Wratten, as the main means of communication between Apaches and whites, was kept busy during the weeks the Indians spent in San Antonio, and he went out of his way to help where help was needed. On October 20 he made an earnest appeal, through the commanding officer, to the War Department in Washington on behalf of his friend An-nan-dia, who was being sent to Fort Pickens with Geronimo instead of to Fort Marion, where his wife and family were being held. He had not gone out with Geronimo but had joined the malcontents later when he was convinced that his life was in danger at San Carlos. Wratten thought highly of him and made a strong plea in his behalf:

When I went into the camp in Old Mexico, just previous to the surrender, he was the first one to come forward to meet me and said that he was very sorry that he had ever left the reservation and did so because he was afraid of his life . . . .

He has always been a sober and industrious man constantly at work performing any kind of work he can get. Never plays cards or gambles and has been studying English very hard . . . . I am induced to make this appeal for personal reasons, as An-nan-dia saved my life when it was attempted by another Indian for the performance of my duty as an employee of the Government.

Clemency, Wratten suggested, "would have an extremely beneficial effect on the rest of the tribe and stimulate them at Fort Marion to adopt civilized means of obtaining a living and that it would be an act of justice to An-nan-dia and his squaw."

General Stanley forwarded Wratten's letter with the comment that the contents were "perfectly true to my knowledge" and added the recommendation that it be given "favorable consideration." The appeal was, nevertheless, denied.[10]

Jasper Kanseah, one of the captives, told Mrs. Eve Ball of an incident that happened in San Antonio:

They held us in San Antonio . . . . They put us in a camp under guard. George Wratten was with us. He was a White Eye but a good

George Wratten and his friend An-nan-dia, Fort Pickens.

man, a true man. He was our interpreter and did not lie about what Geronimo said as Mickey Free did.

We had tents and blankets but no arms. We had food. But every minute we expected to be taken out and shot. Nobody said it aloud. Geronimo had been promised that he would not die by bullets (by Usen, the Apache God), but the rest had not.

One day Mr. Wratten came to Geronimo (he was my uncle too), and he said, "Well, Geronimo, I have done all I can for you but I am afraid they are going to kill you and all your men. Maybe the women too. General Miles put you on the train. Now the President and Secretary of War have authorized him to do so. And they don't know what to do. It looks like the easiest out for both is for you all to be killed trying to escape. I will not see you shot down unarmed. In my tent I have some weapons. And if attacked you are to use them."

"I will use them," promised Geronimo, "I will protect my people if I live. For myself I do not fear for I have the word of Usen. Who is the White Nantan to think he can pit his power against that of Usen?"

"I hope you are right," replied Mr. Wratten, "but I think some good weapons will help a lot."

That night we did not sleep well. And the next morning Mr. Wratten came again. "Well, Geronimo, I guess you are right," he said. "Word came during the night that you are to be put back on the train and taken to Florida."

Geronimo nodded and smiled. "Usen," he said.[11]

On the forty-second day after arriving at San Antonio, the Apache prisoners were on their way to a new and strange land. On October 25 they reached Pensacola, where the women and children were put on a train which would take them to Fort Marion and the main body of the exiles, numbering over 400. The fifteen men, including Geronimo, who had surrendered to General Miles were sent to Fort Pickens, an abandoned fortress on an island near Pensacola where they were to be kept "under close custody." Special Orders no. 149 directed that "Under instructions of the division commander, Interpreter George Wratten will accompany the prisoners to Fort Pickens.[12] On December 8 he was officially transferred to the AAQM at Fort Barrancas, Florida, the Army post near the Fort. "His services are indispensable with the captive Indians at Fort Pickens," said

Fort Pickens, Santa Rosa Island, Pensacola, Florida.

the correspondence, "as he is the only person in that vicinity that can speak their language."[13]

Fort Pickens occupied the western tip of Santa Rosa Island at the eastern entrance to Pensacola Harbor. It was a pentagonal stone structure, built in 1834, with small rooms or cells in which the prisoners had their quarters. In 1886 it was not occupied or cared for and was badly in need of a cleanup, but it could be made livable. On November 30 the post commander reported that Wratten was taking charge. "His services are very necessary as he explains everything, issues rations and clothing under Lieutenant [Charles P.] Parker's direction. He is a most excellent and valuable man in every way. The Indians say they are well satisfied and want to do what is required of them."[14]

The Indians were anything but satisfied, but Wratten told them they had to make the best of their situation, and they did. Early in January Captain Loomis L. Langdon, the officer in charge, reported that the men were well supplied with food and clothing and were "neat and orderly in person, rooms and cooking."

[103]

They are worked six hours a day policing the fort. When it is remembered that Fort Pickens has not been garrisoned since the war, it will be readily understood that the parade, ramparts, ditch, glacis and ramps must be overgrown with weeds, grass, and trees .... Nearly all the growth has been removed by these Indians who labor faithfully and cheerfully under the direction of Lieutenant Charles P. Parker, 2nd Artillery, aided by Mr. Wratten, the interpreter.

The only one who did any complaining was Geronimo and he "was rebuked by Natchez, the Chief .... Lieut. Parker officially reports that not once has the least sign of discontent or insubordination been shown .... They entertain hopes of seeing their families, and this has probably some weight with them."[15] Captain Langdon recommended that the families be reunited at Pickens, but the men had to live alone for a few months longer.

Meanwhile George Wratten was doing his best for them and petitioning Washington for better treatment of particular individuals. One of these was Mangus, a respected leader who had been rounded up with the main party at San Carlos and sent off from Holbrook, Arizona. Near Coolidge, Kansas, he had attempted to escape by jumping through a car window but had been recaptured and confined with the renegades at Fort Pickens. George Wratten wrote to the commanding officer at Fort Barrancas in his behalf, explaining his conduct:

The colored soldiers who were guarding him were constantly aiming their guns at him and threatening to kill him. He thought they were going to do so and the constant repetition of the above frightened him so that he jumped from the car window. They also gave him to understand that the women belonged to them and pointed out which ones they were to take; and, as well as he knows, force them to subject to their passion.

His wife was also one of the party and it made him feel bad to see her treated so. The threats with the guns were made while he was ironed; two days afterwards he jumped from the car believing he was to be killed.[16]

The letter had no effect. On December 29 Lieutenant T. J. Clay answered the complaint: "Mangus and all the other Indians were treated with great kindness and consideration .... The complaint of Mangus is puerile and frivolous in the extreme." Mangus was locked up with Geronimo and his group.

Relief was in sight in the spring of 1887. General P. H. Sheridan, the supreme commander, recommended that the Indians at Fort Marion be transferred to Mt. Vernon Barracks, Alabama. The post, he said, was "perfectly healthy" and its 2163 acres would permit the Indians "to be taught agriculture and to support themselves."[17] Captain John G. Bourke, who had been General Crook's trusted aide, was sent to inspect the site late in April and reported that although the soil was poor, the fort was "one of the prettiest posts in the Army," set among pine trees thirty miles from Mobile. Swamps lay between the site and the coast, but he considered the climate healthy.[18]

In that same month of April, 1887, the families of the prisoners at Fort Pickens were allowed to join them, and the rest of those at Fort Marion were removed to Mount Vernon Barracks.

Geronimo's group were naturally much happier now that their families had come to them, but of course they still wanted to be free. They had George Wratten write a letter to General Stanley in San Antonio reminding him of what he had promised them:

You told them they would be here no longer than a year at the outside and the year is almost up.... They would like to know when they are going to see the good land and farms Gen'l Miles told them about.

They have behaved better under the circumstances than any other lot of people would have, I think.

Stanley kept the letter for three months "as I doubted the propriety of my expressing an opinion upon its contents." He finally forwarded it to Headquarters, Department of the Missouri, with the notation, "I think that the time may come when it would be merciful to restore these people to their tribe at Mount Vernon Barracks .... I am convinced that promises were made to induce them to surrender, which were afterwards so modified, as to amount to bad faith."[19] In due time the government listened, and in May of 1888 the prisoners at Fort Pickens were allowed to join the rest of the Apaches at Mount Vernon. George Wratten came with them. Sam Bowman, who had served as interpreter when the move to Mount Vernon was made, had asked for leave to do some visiting in New Mexico and had not come back. George had the job all to himself.

He found that considerable progress had been made by the 347 Apaches already there. Thirty-eight log cabins had been erected and more were under construction, roads had been repaired, and Assistant Post Surgeon Captain Walter Reed, who was much interested in the welfare of the Indians, reported "General health good."[20] The damp climate was bad for desert people, however, and tuberculosis was already taking its toll.

It was at this time that George took an Apache wife. She was known only as Annie. They were married according to Apache custom, probably without any ceremony, and began living together in the Apache village. The Indians celebrated with a four-day feast.[21] There were two children: Amy, born October 10, 1890, and Blossom, born January 25, 1893. In that year George's widowed mother came out from Albuquerque to be with him. He built a house for her in Mount Vernon and she lived in it for six months. Addie Cannon, later George's sister-in-law, surmised that "she was dissatisfied because of no entertainment and possibly because he was at that time living in the Indian village with his Apache wife and two little daughters. His mother, like many of the Wrattens, was naturally restless. Too, she was not accustomed to that kind of life. She could not tolerate the snubs of the blue-bloods of Mount Vernon, either. She went back west to Arizona."

While all this was going on, George went about his duties as interpreter, teacher and superintendent of reservation activities. His future sister-in-law, Eva Mae McGee of Eunice, Louisiana, described some of his activities:

George taught Geronimo how to make walking sticks. Geronimo would put his name on the walking sticks and charge the tourists $1. If you'd ask, "Why a dollar?" or "How come not fifty cents?" Geronimo would say, "Put name is worth dollar."

The Indians were located in a permanent settlement on a ridge about half a mile west of the military post .... Each family was provided with a comfortable home, but they would not live in them. They preferred their own tents or wickiups out in the yard.

Problems of discipline, says John P. Clum, writing in the *Arizona Historical Review*, were practically eliminated by making soldiers out of the Apache men.

Company I of the 12th Infantry, USA, has been enlisted from these Indians, which is commanded by Captain W. W. Wotherspoon, and Naiche is the first sergeant. The company quarters, mess hall, amusement room, and gymnasium are located on the same ridge with the houses, and form part of the Indian village....

There is a guardhouse at the settlement, and all refractory Indians are arrested by the Indian soldiers and all prisoners are guarded by them....

These Indian prisoners of war are virtually on parole. They are not confined or guarded (as one would expect), and are allowed to come and go when and where they please, provided only that their conduct is proper.[22]

The great problem was sickness, mostly dysentery and tuberculosis, but whiskey, sold by suppliers just outside the reservation, was a growing problem. The death rate was so high and other problems were so serious that individuals and organizations concerned about Indian welfare were active almost from the beginning in trying to find a better place for the prisoners to live. Herbert Welsh of the Indian Rights Association recommended land in Virginia. Professor G. C. Painter of the Indian Rights Commission favored Wilmington, North Carolina. General George Crook, who visited the reservation in January, 1890, strongly supported Fort Sill, Oklahoma. There was much talk but very little action.[23]

The most elaborate survey was ordered by General O. O. Howard, commanding the Headquarters Division of the Missouri. His son, First Lieutenant Guy Howard, submitted a detailed report on December 23, 1889. He pointed out the high death rate and noted that a fourth of those who had come to

Florida in 1886 were already dead. He recommended immediate location of a suitable tract of land and removal to it of all the Indians by March 1, 1890. "Another year's delay would be criminal." He named Fort Sill in the Indian Territory as the best location.[24] President Benjamin Harrison asked the Congress to take action, but the Apaches had to wait three more years for their new home.

George Wratten went among his Indian friends counseling patience as Major William Sinclair noted in his official report, dated December 31, 1889:

That they have behaved remarkably well (far better than the same number of whites and blacks would have done under the circumstances) is very true, but this, I think is largely due to the influence of their Interpreter (George M. Wratten), who has always urged upon them that it is only by their exemplary conduct that they can look forward to any better recognition by the government.[25]

As the man in charge of the Indians, George could not expect to escape criticism, and he was in trouble more than once. In 1889, for example, while Major Sinclair was in charge, an Apache named Go-clay got drunk and George disciplined him. Go-clay, however, stood in well with the people at headquarters, and they came to his defense. Sophie Shepard, the new teacher, complained to the Secretary of War on April 17.

Go-clay, it seems, drank some whiskey—"once"—he says and went home and went to bed respectably. He took it because he "felt sick" and could not eat, so he says; but Mr. Wratten thought otherwise and I dare say Go-clay was in plain English drunk. At any rate he is deprived of his position as Indian Guard and has been sentenced to work on the road. He is in despair, saying he "went long without drinking." He "work hard when he was in Arizona and here and now Mr. Wratten says he bad man; can never go back to Arizona."

Major Sinclair, who by this time had been replaced by Lieutenant Wotherspoon and was living in Boston, wrote in his turn that Go-clay "acted as assistant in the daily issue of rations and other stores required for their use—and for about six months he was the only interpreter" (this was before George

This 1893 photograph shows Apache leaders at Mount Vernon Barracks, Alabama. From left: Chihuahua, Naiche, Loco, Nana, Geronimo.

arrived at Mount Vernon). Go-clay was obviously a favorite. Even Mrs. Daisy Sinclair, the Major's wife, sent a plea with her husband's, dated July 6. "Mr. Wratten, of whom Miss Shepard speaks," she said, "is the interpreter, and I have always thought him a little bit jealous of Go-clay. Let the poor man go back to his people."[26]

Lieutenant Wotherspoon, sitting in judgment, approved Wratten's action.

About the same time, in the summer of 1889, George was attacked from a different direction—by the superintendent of the Carlisle Indian School. The Apache children at the school were dying at an alarming rate. George kept in touch with them by letter, tried to get some of them to come home and help their aging parents, and heard their complaints. He learned in June, 1889, that the superintendent had scattered out seventy-six children on farms and in families in the neighborhood— had kept only fourteen in school. These scattered children received wages of $5 to $10.50 a month and were allowed sometimes to keep only fifty cents per month of the money. George wrote letters of protest to people who might take action. The superintendent retaliated with sharp words and tried to get George removed.

The interpreter at Mount Vernon Barracks, George M. Wratten, is a person not calculated to advance the interests of the Indians nor our relations with them. He is in the habit of writing for the Indians there, discontented letters, in which I see more of the Interpreter than of the Indians themselves. Two or three of the boys who have been here a sufficient length of time to acquire the English language and proper habits of industry, with reasonable ideas of their own and their people's relations to the whites, sent to Mount Vernon Barracks as Interpreters and helpers and the discharge of Mr. Wratten, would benefit the service in every way.[27]

The seriousness of the situation at Carlisle was revealed when the superintendent requested that "orders be given to the Commanding Officer at Mount Vernon barracks to receive 7 prisoners, girls, now at Carlisle to be returned to their parents ... they will die of consumption if not removed." Special Orders no. 123 directed the commanding officer to receive them and a few days later an ambulance brought them to the village. Their parents lifted them out and "carried them to George Wratten to be counted, and then brought them home."[28]

George continued to get good reports from his superiors. Lieutenant Wotherspoon wrote on January 31, 1891, "George Wratten continues to do an excellent job in his supervision of the Indian work and his proper interpretation of the needs and anxieties of the Indians."

Through the early nineties George went about his business undisturbed. Christmas, 1893, was a specially happy time. The holiday was celebrated appropriately with a tree for the school children. George made his usual appearance dressed as Santa Claus and distributed candy and gifts to each Indian child as the group sat around one of the beautiful tall southern pine trees. New Year's came and went and in February, 1894, George was reported as in charge of removing trees and repairing roads. Then in April trouble came from an unexpected source. Geronimo appealed to Major G. B. Russell, commanding the post, to have George Wratten removed. Russell reacted appropriately.

I notified Geronimo to appear at my office on April 1st with any witnesses to facts, and with interpreters of his own selection.

I did not permit a general talk, or "pow-wow," which among Indians is intended primarily for the eclat of their individual consistency; but called each witness in separately. Geronimo said he asked General Miles to send George Wratten with the Apaches at the time of the surrender and seemed to think George was working for him. He told Wratten that "he had been getting from him (Geronimo) much money!" Wratten replied that he got his money from the government.[29]

Among other things, Geronimo said that "If Indians speak to Wratten, he says about three words, and tells the Indians to shut their mouths and go away." Other witnesses did not help Geronimo's case very much but one of them said he had known Wratten to kick a drunken Indian woman.

Given an opportunity to answer the charges, George replied as follows:

It is true that I am very many times compelled to tell Indians to stop talking, to "shut up." It is almost impossible for one of them to confine himself to the matter at issue, and if I were to let each one come to me and talk till he got tired, I would spend all my time in an endless "pow-wow," but no one can truthfully say that I ever refuse to hear anything in reason .... That I have ever kicked or struck with my fist an Indian woman is false, and the charge cannot be sustained by the evidence.[29]

Lieutenant C. C. Ballou endorsed Wratten's reply:

The complaint by Geronimo was probably made in the hope of having Mr. Wratten succeeded as interpreter by one of the Apaches recently dismissed from Carlisle, Pa. Mr. Wratten's honesty, patience, fidelity and capability are too well known to require any comment from me.[30]

The affair caused a flurry of correspondence. Captain W. W. Wotherspoon, formerly in command at the post, wrote about it to the Secretary of War on May 11, 1894:

I am convinced that the post commander is correct in believing the complaint frivolous. I have known Mr. Wratten for four years during which time he was under my command, and I have never known of a single instance of harsh treatment to either men or women. On the contrary, he is always kind and inclined to leniency .... In my long experience in the Army, I have never known a more faithful, honest, reliable and fearless man than Mr. Wratten, nor one whose judgment in dealing with the Indians was more sound. His functions at Mount Vernon are not limited to the duties of interpreter. Indeed that part of his duty is about the least important. He is a skilled farmer, an excellent mechanic, both as a carpenter and smith, and has been of great value in training the Indians. His knowledge of the Indian character has been of the greatest value. I do not believe there is anyone who could take his place....
I think I understand the cause of Geronimo's jealousy very well; he is forever wanting to have talks or "pow-wows," simply to magnify his importance, and as my whole efforts for a long time were bent on reducing that importance, I refused repeatedly to hear him talk in anything like a council .... I only once gave him a chance to talk as he wished; on that occcasion without consulting me, he gathered

[112]

about all the Indians together to hear him; it was simply to make an impression upon them and the substance of it was that as I had failed to stop the Indians drinking, I should employ him at a salary to do so. I refused to grant his request and to show his power he got drunk the next day. I was prepared for this, and at once put him in the guardhouse like any other drunkard, and made him work with the camp prisoners four or five days; from that time on he has taken a dislike for Mr. Wratten, for his power was broken.[31]

The net result was that George Wratten was highly commended for his work and retained in his position. Geronimo nursed his grudge, however, and when he dictated his life story to S. M. Barrett in 1906, he showed his dislike and said things about Wratten that were not true. "He has always had trouble with the Indians," Geronimo said, "because he mistreated them. One day, an Indian, while drunk, stabbed Mr. Wratten with a little knife. The officer in charge took the part of Mr. Wratten and sent the Indian to prison."[32] It was Sam Bowman, George's predecessor at Mount Vernon, who was stabbed.

By the end of September, 1894, plans had been completed for abandoning the village at Mount Vernon and transferring all but a few of the Indians to a new home at Fort Sill, Oklahoma. Captain H. L. Scott was in charge of the move. He had come to Mount Vernon to talk to the Apaches and see how they felt about it. They told him they did not like living in a place "no longer than your thumb nail on which the trees were so thick that you would have to climb up to the top of a tall pine if you wanted to see the sun; and when you climbed down and went somewhere to sit and rest yourself, there was always something waiting to bite you."[33] Oklahoma would be better. Scott promised to take them where they could see the sun without climbing a tree and could even see mountains again. He persuaded the Kiowas and Comanches already on the reservation that the newcomers would live only on land near the post and would not make trouble for them. The white people of the area, however, were unreconciled. The editor of the Mingus, Oklahoma, *Minstrel* wrote: "Yes, here we go to see the king of murderers and prince of fiery destruction now made glorious by the sentimental adulation of insane freaks and misguided philanthropists. The old devil [Geronimo] should have been hung fifteen years ago."[34]

There was nothing glorious about Geronimo and his people when they arrived at Fort Sill on October 7, 1894. They had traveled by way of Fort Worth on a special train to Rush Springs, and from that point had made a thirty-mile trip to their new home by wagon. On arriving at Fort Sill, they were assigned a place two miles northeast of the post, where Geronimo later had his village, on a little knoll. It was too late in the season for them to attempt to erect houses and they put up wickiups in the brush.

They were poor, bedraggled, and pathetic. They had no livestock, not even dogs, and very little clothing and few personal belongings. They did, however, have their friend and interpreter, George Wratten, who was officially assigned to Lieutenant John A. Harmon, the quartermaster at Fort Sill. In the spring Captain Scott put everybody to work, under George's supervision, cutting pickets and putting up houses. George divided them into groups and assigned them to small villages scattered over the reservation. In his 1955 letter Jason Betzinez wrote:

> In order to utilize the most suitable locations where wood, water and grazing land were available, Scott and George Wratten divided the tribes into small groups, each to live in a village. It was decided to retain as far as possible the normal life of the family groupings, each with its own head man who would be enlisted as a scout, a U. S. Indian scout, who would act as supervisor of his own band.

Wratten chose the head man for each village and Geronimo himself was enlisted as a scout, although he was old and practically worthless, except as a show piece to satisfy the insatiable curiosity of the public. Naiche continued to be the hereditary chief, although he was not allowed to exert any influence. Wratten supervised the Indians as they cut and baled hay and cut Kaffir corn (which Captain Scott had introduced to the west). They also grew melons and several kinds of vegetables. Later on they raised cattle. Wratten could have grazed cattle of his own with the Indian herd, but he thought it would be

[114]

Top: wickiups at Fort Sill used during the winter of 1894. Bottom: Geronimo, Chihuahua, Nana, Loco, and Jolsanny at Fort Sill.

wrong. He lived on his $100 a month, supplementing his income by operating the trading post. His extra work never brought him any extra pay.

George used his trading post to start some of the Apache boys on the road to education. Eugene Chihuahua was one. In an interview with Eve Ball on the Mescalero Reservation he told how George had given him a job in the store "and from words on boxes and bags taught me how to read. He taught me how to write by making lists of things. And he taught me how to count and make change. I wanted to know those things that those children who were sent to Carlisle were being taught, and Mr. Wratten helped me to do that. George said to me, 'From now on I will speak English to you and you ask me what I mean if you don't understand.' After that I learned English rapidly."[35]

Meanwhile George was planning to marry again. Before he left Mount Vernon he had separated from his Indian wife, following tribal custom, and she had married Talbot Gooday, who later became prominent on the Mescalero Reservation in New Mexico. George's new interest was Julia Elizabeth Cannon, who belonged to one of the first families of Mount Vernon.

When George arrived with the prisoners of war in 1888, Bessie was only ten years of age, and of course there was no thought of what the future might bring. He was a romantic figure, however, and it is no wonder that Bessie kept her eyes and thoughts on him for the remainder of her life. In 1894 George went with the Apaches to Fort Sill, but in 1896, when Bessie was eighteen, he came back and asked her father for her hand in marriage. Bessie's sister told what happened.

Eva Mae was in the living room when George asked their father if he could marry Bessie. They argued and argued. All can understand why. No doubt for several reasons, but mainly because she was so very young—just eighteen. He was much older. She knew not a thing about his life, that is the hardships, etc. She was one of the most popular belles in the County of Mobile—had never known what it was to keep house, cook, etc. She had never been away from home and she would have to go immediately to the frontier post of Fort Sill and live among the Indians, who had only a few years previously been

[116]

George Wratten

George and Bessie's children at Fort Sill.

Bessie Cannon Wratten

[117]

complete savages. He had had an Apache wife and still had two young daughters living in the Village with him. He had become a Master Mason and she and the entire contingent of Cannons and Duclouxs were devout Catholics—ad infinitum . . . .

Mr. Cannon told George if she was of the same frame of mind, in love with him and wanted to marry him, after she became twenty-one within three years, he could have her.[36]

So in three years George returned to claim his bride. They were married on October 31, 1899, in Mount Vernon by a Catholic priest, Father Leonard.

During the three years George waited for Bessie, he built a house for her at Fort Sill near the old quarry and she told him by letter what colors to paint the rooms.

It was not long after the move to Fort Sill that Geronimo became a side-show attraction. Sometimes on his trips George went along to look after him. The excursions began in 1898 at the Trans-Mississippi and International Exhibition at Omaha, and after that Geronimo was a frequent visitor to fairs, exhibitions, reunions, and public functions of all kinds. He was a great drawing card and made money by selling pictures of himself, bows and arrows, buttons off his shirt, and even his hat. His success went to his head and made him feel that he was better than the other Apaches, although it was he who had brought all their misery and deprivation on them. In the summer of 1901 he was at the Pan-American Exposition in Buffalo and then came a round of local appearances in Oklahoma. In 1904 he was a featured attraction at the Louisiana Purchase Exposition, with George Wratten in charge.

The biggest event of all came the following year, 1905, when Geronimo traveled to Washington at the invitation of President Theodore Roosevelt to ride in the parade at the second inaugural—one of half a dozen Indian leaders from western tribes. Geronimo's favorite horse was shipped in for the occasion. John P. Clum, who was working as a newspaperman at the time, had this to say about the spectacle:

The grand climax of the comedy came on March 4, 1905 . . . . Westward, down Pennsylvania Avenue, between a phalanx of half a

[118]

Geronimo rides as a celebrity in the inaugural parade, 1905.

million cheering citizens, came the Inaugural Parade. In the lead "Teddy" himself, doffing his silk topper, smiling broadly this way and that. Next, the Guard of Honor, then an Army band. Geronimo in that parade was Public Hero Number Two.

It was my privilege, as a newspaper correspondent, to sit near President Roosevelt in the stand in front of the White House while he reviewed his own parade. To him I said, "Why did you select Geronimo to march in your own parade, Mr. President? He is the greatest single-handed murderer in American history." To which he characteristically replied, "I wanted to give the people a good show." Well, he gave it to them.

Eskiminzin, Tauelclyee, Goodah, Sneezer—red men who always had been loyal to the whiteman's government, who had risked their lives to protect their white brothers, who had striven to the limits of their understanding, for peace and justice, who had ever heard of them?[37]

Clum could well have mentioned one more—George Wratten, the Apaches' best friend, who had accompanied Geronimo to Washington.

[119]

The day after the parade Dr. S. M. Huddleson interviewed George and Geronimo at the Capitol Hotel, as already mentioned, and Wratten commented on his relations with the old man.

"The best way to get along with an Indian is to make him a pal. I had pretty near to make *that* Indian all over again. He had absolutely no education, no manners, and no civilized idea of cleanliness. I taught him as I would a wee boy in school. What civilization or education he has, he owes to me. He will print his name for you if you ask him. He is very fond of doing that." Geronimo here interposed, smilingly drew his name on a card, and proffered it to me, thereby proving that he understood more English than one might give him credit for.[38]

On February 4, 1908, George resigned his post and went back to Mount Vernon to live. Bessie was lonesome among strangers and wanted to be near her people, so George decided to try farming and cattle raising back in Alabama. He made a home for his family in the old post office building and leased land across the river from town. For two years he struggled against heavy odds, but just as he was beginning to get well established, the river flooded and swept everything away. His best friend, whom he had counted on, was unwilling to help him and the people of Mount Vernon treated him shamefully. At the end of the second year he gave up and went back to his old job on the reservation, to the only friends he knew—to the Apaches, to his Army-officer superiors, to the only people who knew and understood him. Geronimo died while he was away, and that may have influenced his decision to return.

By this time his health was going bad. His son Joe in an interview on March 1, 1969, revealed what had gone wrong.

The way I heard it, he was catching a horse in a corral and the ground was parched and hard. He tripped on a rope and it threw him on that hard ground on the base of his spine. I don't believe Daddy had ever been thrown.

The Indians had cattle which ran all over that place. There wasn't any stock law then but they had their cattle on their range, acres and acres of it. I guess they had a fence somewhere. They kept pretty good control of them. And Daddy was out all the time, even when he was sick and couldn't ride a horse, he was out in a buggy.

You see his back trouble was at the base of his spine. He couldn't sit. He wore, before he got down in bed, a solid steel brace from his hips up under his arms, and then after that they put a cast all around him, also from his hips to his arm pits.

What he had was tuberculosis of the spine. He went to the hospital and had an operation which did no good, and when he came home they put him in a tent in the yard and had a male nurse for him. Joe said that "with a cast brace and all, he would sit up as best he could and interpret for the Indians, for the soldiers and for the commanding officer, when they came over for that purpose."

He died on June 23, 1912. On June 24 the Lawton newspaper noted his passing, calling him a "friend and associate of the Apache Indians," known particularly "for the part he played in effecting the capture of Geronimo." Bessie Wratten took the children back to Mount Vernon, where she married again and died on February 22, 1922.

George's first wife, Annie Gooday, severely burned by an explosion in her kitchen, died on the reservation a year after George's death, leaving seven children besides George's daughters Amy and Blossom.

It was many years before the half brothers and sisters were reunited. Amy died before communication was established. Blossom survived, and she and Amy's daughter Mildred Cleghorn contributed many facts to the record in interviews on the Mescalero Reservation in 1959. Bessie's children are proud of their Apache relatives and commend them for their insistence on full education for each one.

George did not live to see his dream of freedom for his Indians realized, but it came true in 1913, the year after his death, when the Apaches at Fort Sill were given the choice of receiving an allotment of land or transportation to a new home on the Mescalero Reservation in New Mexico. His last days were spent in deep frustration because of his failure to help his Apaches remove their chains as prisoners of war. He never stopped resenting General Miles' broken promises, the notoriety

Albert Wratten, wearing a white shirt, and Blossom Hazaous, his half-sister, pose with tribal friends at the Mescalero Reservation.

given to Geronimo to the exclusion of Naiche, the real chief, and others, the shameful competition of Miles, Lawton, and even such a ridiculous figure as Tom Horn for laurels they never earned.

He could have written a true account of the Apaches and their history and set the record straight, but he would never talk much about such matters and would never write or allow to be written his views on the entire sordid story of the treatment of the captives or the scrambling for credit for bringing them in from Mexico. All during the controversy between the supporters of Miles and Crook he undoubtedly had his deep convictions, but he also needed to keep his job as interpreter and supervisor at Fort Sill. Had he spoken out as did Frank P. Bennett (former Chief of Scouts and his companion in Mexico) in 1890, he would no doubt have shared Bennett's fate. While Frank was working as a watchman in the Post Office Department in

Washington, he printed a letter in the *Washington Star* on February 25 calling for justice and recognition for Gatewood, and he lost his job—"no reason given or charges preferred"— on March 5. Wratten had a wife and children to support, was in ill health, and was deeply concerned about the plight of his Apaches. It was wise for him to keep silent. That, however, does not keep his son from trying to explain the part he played in an important aspect of American history.

George Wratten's efforts to help his Indians were certainly not in vain. After devoting the best part of his short life to their welfare, he was laid to rest in an honored part of the Fort Sill Post Cemetery, with a red granite marker to remind visitors that though he was not given the place in history commensurate with his contribution, he had done his best.

NOTES

[1]Addie M. Cannon to Albert E. Wratten, December 5, 1957. Addie remembered George as he looked when he arrived at Mount Vernon, Alabama, in 1888 when he was twenty-three.

[2]Dates of Wratten's enlistment and transfers are probably from family records. Some scattered references about civilian employees of the post quartermasters are available in Record Group 92, National Archives (for example, "Report of Persons and Articles Employed and hired at Fort Cummings, New Mexico," July, 1882, and August, 1882, which dates Wratten's enlistment and first transfer), but Albert Wratten is not likely to have seen such documents since he did not visit Washington.

[3]Hugh L. Scott, Major General, U. S. A. Ret., *Some Memories of a Soldier* (New York: Century, 1928), p. 91.

[4]Wirt Davis, Captain, 4th Cavalry, Fort Lowell, A. T., to Captain C. S. Roberts, 17th Infantry, March 20, 1886 (typescript), Gatewood Collection, Arizona Historical Society, Tucson, Box 5, Folder 19.

[5]Dr. S. M. Huddleson to Charles Gatewood, Washington, D. C., June 27, 1925, Gatewood Collection, Box 5, Folder 19.

[6]*Ibid.* Wratten's account agrees, in outline, with Lieutenant Charles B. Gatewood's account in this issue and with Morris E. Opler's "A Chiricahua's Account of the Geronimo Campaign of 1886," *New Mexico Historical Review,* vol. 13 (October, 1938), pp. 337-386.

[7]Jess Hayes, *Apache Vengeance* (University of New Mexico Press, 1954), p. 2.

[8]*San Antonio Express*, September 11, 1886, quoted by David M. Goodman, "Apaches as Prisoners of War," unpublished Ph. D. dissertation, Texas Christian University, 1968, p. 32.

[9]*Ibid.*, p. 53.

[10]Wratten to D. S. Stanley, October 20, 1886, Record Group 94, Microcopy no. 689, "Letters Received by the Office of the Adjutant General, Main Series 1881-1889, Selected List of Consolidated Files, rolls 173-202 (File 1066, AGO 1883), hereafter referred to as Consolidated Files.

[11]Eve Ball gives a shorter version of this episode in *Indeh* (Provo, Utah: Brigham Young University Press, 1980), p. 131.

[12]Consolidated Files, Special Orders No. 149.

[13]*Ibid.*, December 8, 1886.

[14]*Ibid.*, November 30, 1886.

[15]*Ibid.*, January 7, 1887.

[16]*Ibid.*, October 3, 1887.

[17]*Ibid.*, May 12, 1888.

[18]*Ibid.*, April 19, 1887.

[19]*Ibid.*, October 3, 1887, January 4, 1888.

[20]*Ibid.*, May 12, 1888.

[21]Eve Ball included this interview in *Indeh*, pp. 155-156.

[22]John P. Clum, "Geronimo," *Arizona Historical Review*, vol. 3 (October, 1938), pp. 36-37.

[23]Senate Executive Document no. 35, 51 Cong., 2nd Sess., pp. 1-8; Consolidated Files, June 29, 1889.

[24]Senate Executive Document 35, pp. 38-39.

[25]Consolidated Files, December 31, 1889.

[26]*Ibid.*, June 28, 1888. Go-clay, from San Carlos, said he was not a prisoner but had come voluntarily in 1886. His return was approved on September 4, 1890.

[27]*Ibid.*, May 24, 1889.

[28]Goodman, "Apaches as Prisoners of War," p. 167.

[29]Consolidated Files, April 4, 1894.

[30]*Ibid.*, endorsement on back of Wratten's statement.

[31]*Ibid.*, May 24, 1894.

[32]S. M. Barrett, *Geronimo's Story of His Life* (New York: Duffield, 1906), p. 179; Goodman, "Apaches as Prisoners of War," p. 124; Consolidated Files, August 8, 1887.

[33]Hugh Lenox Scott, *Some Memories of a Soldier*, pp. 182-183. Angie Debo in *Geronimo: The Man, His Time, His Place* (Norman: University of Oklahoma Press, 1976, 1982), pp. 358-365, describes the negotiations and the move to Fort Sill.

[34]*Mingus Minstrel*, October 5, 1894. The article is quoted in Wilbur S. Nye, *Carbine and Lance* (Norman: University of Oklahoma Press, 1937), p. 297.

[35]Eugene Chihuahua, interview with Eve Ball, sent to Albert E. Wratten at an unspecified date and printed in *Indeh*, p. 166.

[36]Albert does not identify the relative (probably one of Bessie's sisters) who provided the information.

[37]John P. Clum, "Geronimo," *New Mexico Historical Review*, vol. 3 (April, 1938), pp. 254-255.

[38]S. M. Huddleson to Charles Gatewood, June 27, 1925, *op. cit.*

CREDITS—The U.S. Signal Corps photograph on page 93 (top) and that on page 109 are from the National Archives; on page 93 (bottom) from the Gledhill Collection, Arizona Historical Society, Tucson; on page 117 (top and bottom) from the Wratten Collection, AHS; on page 99 and 115 (bottom) from general collections, AHS; on page 95, 101, and 115 (top) from the Fort Sill Museum, Fort Sill, OK; on page 103 courtesy of Mrs. Albert Wratten and the Gulf Island Interpreters; on page 122 courtesy of Mrs. Albert Wratten; on page 119 from the Bureau of American Ethnology Collection, Smithsonian Institution National Anthropological Archives.

THE END OF THE APACHE WARS—
THE BASIC WRITINGS

These books and articles can be found in many good public libraries and in any university library.

Alexander Adams, *Geronimo*. New York: Putnam, 1971; New York: Berkeley Medallion (soft cover), 1972.

Adams sketches the background of the Apache troubles, beginning with the massacre of Apaches which is supposed (wrongly) to have taken place at Santa Rita del Cobre in 1837 and concluding with the surrender. Geronimo is "the long-misunderstood Apache leader," fighting to save his land from the "white invaders." The book is of little value to serious students but provides a good introduction to the period and the people for casual readers.

Elliot Arnold, *Blood Brother* (fiction). New York: Duell, Sloan & Pearce, 1947; Lincoln, Nebraska: University of Nebraska Press (soft cover), 1979.

In this famous novel, subject of an even-more-famous moving picture, mail-contractor Tom Jeffords becomes a blood brother of the great chief Cochise and marries an Apache girl. There is peace as a result between Apaches and whites until Cochise dies and Jeffords is discredited. The idealization of the Indian owes much to this book.

Eve Ball, "The Apache Scouts: A Chiricahua Appraisal," *Arizona and the West*, vol. 7 (Spring, 1971), pp. 315-328.

"Juh's stronghold in Mexico," *Journal of Arizona History*, vol. 15 (Spring, 1971), pp. 73-84.

Indeh: An Apache Odyssey. Provo, Utah: Brigham Young University Press, 1980 (with Nora Henn and Lynda Sanchez).

Eve Ball, with little training as a historian, did more in the last third of her life to write Apache history from the Indian point of view than any other person. Basing her work on interviews with the survivors of the final struggle, she published three important books and a number of valuable articles. *Indeh*, her last and probably most significant work, assembles these interviews into a chronological account of the Apaches' final tragedy.

S. M. Barrett, ed., *Geronimo's Story of His Life*. New York: Duffield, 1906; New York: Ballantine, 1978 (soft cover).

Barrett, an Oklahoma teacher, persuaded Geronimo to dictate his reminiscences, translated by an English-speaking relative. Geronimo's memory was not always reliable, and he gave himself the best of every episode, but his account is indispensable to an understanding of his career.

Jane Barry, *A Time in the Sun* (fiction). Garden City: Doubleday, 1962.

An Eastern girl en route to marry her soldier fiancé in Arizona is captured by the Chiricahuas. She finds them congenial and marries half-Mexican Joaquín. The white men are now the savages and the Apaches are the truly civilized people.

Jason Betzinez, *I Fought with Geronimo*, ed., W. S. Nye. Harrisburg, Pennsylvania: Stackpole, 1959.

As a child Betzinez lived in Mexico with Geronimo's Apache fugitives before the surrender and went into exile with them. An intelligent, educated, and communicative individual, he gives the best account of what went on from an Indian boy's point of view.

John Bigelow, Jr., *On the Bloody Trail of Geronimo,* ed., Arthur Woodward. Los Angeles: Westernlore Press, 1958.

Lieutenant Bigelow and his "Buffalo Soldiers" did not pursue Geronimo into Mexico in 1885 but guarded the mountain passes near the border. His diary, first published in *Outing* magazine in 1886-1887, reveals much about Army life in the field during the campaigns.

John G. Bourke, *An Apache Campaign in the Sierra Madre.*

New York: Scribner's, 1886; Glorieta, New Mexico: Rio Grande Press, 1958.

On the Border with Crook. New York: Scribner's, 1891; Glorieta, New Mexico: Rio Grande Press, 1971.

As General Crook's trusted aide, Bourke was familiar with all aspects of the campaigns against the Apaches. In the judgment of such historians as Dan L. Thrapp, his books are the ones to start with.

John Bret Harte, "Conflict at San Carlos: The Civilian-Military Struggle for Control, 1882-1885," *Arizona and the West,* vol. 15 (Spring, 1973), pp. 27-44.

"The Strange Case of Joseph C. Tiffany: Indian Agent in Disgrace," *Journal of Arizona History,* vol. 16 (Winter, 1975), pp. 383-404.

In the background of the Apache troubles was the disagreement over who should be in charge at the San Carlos Agency. The legend of the corrupt agent is accepted as truth by historians and novelists. Bret Harte shows that Joseph C. Tiffany, long regarded as the most corrupt of all, was really an inept but well-meaning scapegoat and victim.

Edgar Rice Burroughs, *The War Chief* (fiction). Chicago: McClurg, 1927; London: Methuen, 1928; New York: Ballantine, 1964 (soft cover).

Apache Devil (fiction). Tarzana, California: Burroughs, 1933; New York: Ballantine, 1964 (soft cover); Boston: Gregg, 1978.

Shoz-dí-ji-ji (Black Bear), unaware that he is white, has been adopted by Geronimo, who emerges as a peace-loving gentleman whose great hope is that the whites will some day keep their promises.

Charles Byars, ed., "Gatewood Reports to His Wife from Geronimo's Camp," *Journal of Arizona History,* vol. 7 (Summer, 1966), pp. 76-81.

In his letters from the field Gatewood reveals much that was not included in his official reports, adding a human touch to military history.

John P. Clum, "Geronimo," *New Mexico Historical Review*, vol. 3 (January, 1928), pp. 1-40.

Clum was the brash but efficient young agent at San Carlos (1874-1877), where he created a system of Indian police and offered to manage all the Indians in Arizona if the government would consent. He was the only man ever to capture Geronimo and was foremost among Geronimo haters.

Woodworth Clum, *Apache Agent: The Story of John P. Clum.* Boston: Houghton Mifflin, 1936.

Clum's son tells his story with enthusiasm and with complete trust in his father's recollections. His work is useful if sometimes less than accurate.

Will L. Comfort, *Apache* (fiction). New York: Dutton, 1931.

This much-praised novel about Mangus Colorado, often reprinted, is an outstanding work on the Apaches of the Southwest. It was of first importance in the reversal of white attitudes toward them.

George Crook, *General George Crook: His Autobiography*, ed., Martin F. Schmitt. Norman: University of Oklahoma Press, 1946, 1960.

Crook was unable to continue his reminiscences past 1876, but his views on Apaches, Indian agents, and the situation in Arizona are clearly expressed.

Thomas Cruse, *Apache Days and After*. Caldwell, Idaho: Caxton Printers, 1941.

Cruse as a young officer was involved in Geronimo's early difficulties but was stationed at Fort Stanton at the time of the surrender.

Britton Davis, *The Truth about Geronimo*. New Haven: Yale University Press, 1929; Lincoln, Nebraska: University of Nebraska Press, 1976 (soft cover).

Davis was an officer with Crook's forces in Mexico and gives a lively account of his experiences. His book ranks with Bourke's two volumes as a primary source.

Angie Debo, *Geronimo: The Man, His Time, His Place*. Norman: University of Oklahoma Press, 1976, 1977, 1982 (soft cover).

Debo began collecting material on Geronimo in the 1950s and has produced a definitive biography. She regards him as "a man of essential integrity" who behaved correctly according to his lights, showing intelligence, adaptability, and strength of character.

Odie B. Faulk, *The Geronimo Campaign*. New York: Oxford, 1969.

An excellent summary of all aspects of the campaign against the Apaches and its aftermath by a skilful writer and researcher. Faulk's treatment is even-handed, giving both sides sympathetic treatment.

George MacDonald Fraser, *Flashman and the Redskins* (fiction). New York: Knopf, 1982.

This is a hilarious spoof on the shibboleths and sacred cows of American history. Flashy is a complete cad who is engagingly candid about his sins and weaknesses, which include lying, cheating, and cowardice. He has operated all over the world with the British Army, but this novel brings him to the United States, including the Southwest. He becomes a friend of Geronimo and marries Sonsee-ahrray (her name borrowed from *Blood Brother*), providing a new and original view of both of them.

Charles B. Gatewood, "The Surrender of Geronimo," *Arizona Historical Review*, vol. 4 (April, 1931), pp. 33-44.

This was the first accessible account by Gatewood, though it had appeared in the *Proceedings of the Annual Meeting and Dinner of the Order of the Indian Wars of the United States* (Washington, 1929). It was based on an original handwritten manuscript prepared by the elder Gatewood and edited, with considerable change, by his son, Major Charles B. Gatewood. It appeared again in *The Papers of the Order of Indian Wars* (q. v.) in 1975. The original handwritten version has been transcribed and appears in this issue. A third version, approximately twice as long, was prepared from his father's notes and from documentary research and correspondence by the younger Gatewood, who deposited it with all his other material in the archives of the Arizona Historical Society. It remains unpublished.

[129]

David Michael Goodman, "Apaches as Prisoners of War," Ph.D. dissertation, Texas Christian University, 1968, reproduced electronically by University Microfilms, Ann Arbor, Michigan (no date).

The best account of the Apaches in exile.

William T. Hagan, *The Indian Rights Association: The Herbert Welsh Years.* Tucson: University of Arizona Press, 1985.

Hagan gives a brief but informed account of the efforts by Welsh and the Association to better the condition of the Apaches in Florida and Alabama, pp. 92-96, 143-144.

Herman Hagedorn, *Leonard Wood: A Biography.* 2 vols., New York: Harper, 1931.

Wood, a contract surgeon, was with Lawton's troops in Mexico at the time of the Gatewood-Geronimo conference, helped escort the Indians to Skeleton Canyon, and was present at the surrender. Hagedorn used Wood's diary in recording this early episode in his career.

Will Henry (Henry Wilson Allen), *Chiricahua* (fiction). Philadelphia: Lippincott, 1972; Boston: Gregg, 1978.

Henry is sympathetic with the Apaches without idealizing them. An important character is the White Mountain Apache known as Peaches, who located the fugitives in Mexico for Crook. The novel has won high praise from critics.

Forrestine Cooper Hooker, *When Geronimo Rode* (fiction). New York: Doubleday, 1924.

Daughter of an Army officer, Hooker spent her early years at frontier Army posts during the Apache wars. Her book is fictionized history with emphasis on garrison life and an Army romance. Her opinion of Geronimo is low. She reports the surrender (by letter from her leading man), giving Crawford and Miles most of the credit.

Paul Horgan, *A Distant Trumpet* (fiction). New York: Farrar & Straus, 1960.

Horgan's superior novel of Army life in the West follows the career of Matthew Hazard, who takes the part of Gatewood, and of Major General Alexander Upton Quait, who is Crook with some special eccentricities attached. The surrender of Rainbow's Son (Geronimo) is the climactic event.

[130]

Tom Horn, *Life of Tom Horn: A Vindication*. Denver: Louthan, 1904.

Horn wrote, or helped to write, his autobiography while he was in prison awaiting execution. He was present at Gatewood's conference as one of two interpreters and takes credit for the surrender. All critics agree that his claims are unfounded, but he was there.

Oliver O. Howard, *My Life and Experiences among Our Hostile Indians*. Hartford, Connecticut: A. D. Worthington, 1907.

Howard's agreement with Cochise in 1872 and the appointment of Tom Jeffords as Chiricahua Indian Agent at Cochise's request resulted in four years of peace. The Geronimo campaign followed the collapse of the treaty, the removal of Jeffords, and the attempt to transfer the Chiricahua bands to San Carlos.

Virginia W. Johnson, *The Unregimented General: A Biography of Nelson A. Miles*. Boston: Houghton Mifflin, 1962.

Miles has been a controversial figure since the surrender, for which he took full credit to the indignation of the friends and supporters of Charles B. Gatewood. Johnson is not one of his detractors, giving him high marks for courage and independence.

Harry C. Kramer III, "Tom Jeffords, Indian Agent," *Journal of Arizona History*, vol. 17 (Autumn, 1976), pp. 285-300.

Kramer's essay documents Jeffords's tenure as agent for the Chiricahuas. Jeffords emerges as a man of tact, intelligence, and good will caught in an impossible situation. He defended himself as best he could from unjust criticism, eventually going down to a defeat which led directly to the Geronimo outbreaks.

Frank C. Lockwood, *The Apache Indians*. New York: Macmillan, 1938.

Lockwood's pioneer history of the Apaches and the Apache troubles, though it shows little sympathy for the Indian and takes the Army point of view, is still a valuable work.

Anton Mazzanovich, *Trailing Geronimo*. Privately printed, 1926.

Mazzanovich was with the U. S. Army in Mexico as a packer.

He tells the story from the enlisted man's point of view and stands firmly on the side of Gatewood against the supporters of Lawton and Miles.

Nelson A. Miles, *Personal Recollections and Observations*. Chicago: The Werner Company, 1897.

Miles's reminiscences, covering his whole career, contain his version of the Apache finale. All his subordinates except Gatewood get credit.

Ralph H. Ogle, *Federal Control of the Western Apaches, 1848-1886*. Albuquerque: University of New Mexico Press, 1940.

Although this Ph. D. dissertation has been largely superseded by later works, it is still useful in pointing up the origins of the Apache troubles in the Army-Civilian battle for control of the reservations. The events of 1885-1886 are briefly sketched.

James R. Olson, *Ulzana* (fiction). Boston: Houghton Mifflin, 1973.

Ulzana was a minor Apache chief, leader of a famous raid through Arizona and New Mexico. Olson imagines him as an American businessman in a breechclout, talking American middle-class English and sharing the values of white civilization. It is easy to empathize with him because he is not different from us.

Morris E. Opler, *An Apache Life-Way: The Economic, Social and Religious Institutions of the Chiricahua Indians*. Chicago: The University of Chicago Press, 1941.

Anthropologist Opler writes a nearly definitive account of the Apaches' beliefs, rituals, taboos, etc. Geronimo makes an appearance as shaman. Useful for anyone who wants the basics.

Order of Indian Wars, *The Papers of the Order of Indian Wars* (Introduction by John M. Carroll). Fort Collins, Colorado: Old Army Press, 1975.

Contains papers by Brigadier General James H. Parker (q. v.), Lieutenant Charles B. Gatewood (q. v.), and Lieutenant Thomas J. Clay ("Some Unwritten Incidents of the Geronimo Campaign," pp. 114-116). Clay brought supplies to Lawton

[132]

in Mexico and was nearby when Geronimo agreed to surrender. Clay was a strong supporter of Gatewood: "If it had not been for their confidence in Gatewood, I do not believe they would have surrendered when they did" (p. 115).

Gwendolyn Overton, *The Heritage of Unrest* (fiction). New York: Macmillan, 1901.

Daughter and wife of Army officers, Overton knew the Apaches at close range. Her book, best of the early Apache War novels, shows some sympathy for the Indians and an awareness of their situation. Her heroine is half Apache and has trouble coping with her "taint."

James Parker, *The Old Army: Memories 1872-1918*. Philadelphia: Dorrance & Company, 1929.

Parker, then a lieutenant, was in charge of a small detachment and joined Gatewood when he entered Mexico. He minimizes Gatewood's achievement and claims credit for suggesting to Miles that the peaceful Apaches be sent to Florida.

John Rope, "Experiences of an Indian Scout," recorded by Grenville Goodwin, *Arizona Historical Review*, vol. 3 (April, 1936), pp. 31-73 (second of two installments).

Rope was not curious about politics or tactics, but he has a good deal to say about the way the scouts felt about other things.

C. L. Sonnichsen, "The Ambivalent Apache," *Western American Literature*, vol. 10 (August, 1975); *From Hopalong to Hud: Thoughts on Western Fiction*. College Station: Texas A & M University Press, 1978, pp. 64-82.

Changing images of the Apache as reflected in fiction over the years.

"Who was Tom Jeffords?" *Journal of Arizona History*, vol. 23 (Winter, 1982), pp. 381-406.

This essay attempts to show what sort of person Jeffords really was, taking into account his success with the Apaches and his failure to achieve other usual human goals.

John Upton Terrell, *Apache Chronicle*. New York: World, 1972.

Terrell is a leader in the movement to damn the white man

and elevate the Apache. His indignation is genuine and justified, but he sees only one side of the picture.

Dan L. Thrapp, *Al Sieber: Chief of Scouts.* Norman: University of Oklahoma Press, 1964.

The Conquest of Apacheria. Norman: University of Oklahoma Press, 1967.

General Crook and the Sierra Madre Adventure. Norman: University of Oklahoma Press, 1972.

Juh, an Incredible Indian. El Paso: Texas Western Press, 1973.

Dateline Fort Bowie: Charles Fletcher Lummis Reports on an Apache War. Norman: University of Oklahoma Press, 1979.

Thrapp is the premier student and recorder of the Apache Wars. He is a military historian, inevitably, for the Army left voluminous records and the Apaches did not. Thrapp aims at objectivity, however, and attains as much of it as a white historian can.

John A. Turcheneske, Jr., "The Arizona Press and Geronimo's Surrender," *Journal of Arizona History,* vol. 14 (Summer, 1973), pp. 133-148.

The Territorial newspapers took the lead in spreading panic among the pioneers, screaming for outside help, damning the Army, and calling for the extermination or removal of the Apaches.

Robert M. Utley, *Frontier Regulars: The United States Army and the Indian, 1866-1891.* New York: Macmillan, 1973.

Utley treats the Indian wars without sentimentality or special pleading. He believes that the conflicts were inevitable since neither side understood the motivation of the other.

Charles Marquis Warren, *Only the Valiant* (fiction). Garden City: Doubleday, 1936; New York: Modern Library, 1969.

An excellent early novel about life at a frontier military post. The great Apache leader Tucsos is defeated in a climactic battle at Apache Pass by the use of the first Gatling gun in the Southwest.

Paul I. Wellman, *Broncho Apache* (fiction). Garden City: Doubleday, 1936.

Another excellent novel concentrating on Massai, who escaped from a prison train bound for Florida somewhere west of St. Louis in September, 1886. He made his way back to Arizona in real life and resumed the old raiding style.

Herbert Welsh, *The Apache Prisoners in Fort Marion, St. Augustine, Florida.* Philadelphia: Indian Rights Association, 1887.

Welsh was indefatigable in pressing for justice and a better life for the Apache captives.

Donald E. Worcester, *The Apaches: Eagles of the Southwest.* Norman: University of Oklahoma Press, 1979.

Worcester synthesizes the research that has been done on the Apaches from the beginning. He needs more than one book to tell it all, but he does his best.